# Cultural Crowdfunding: Platform Capitalism, Labour and Globalization

Edited by
Vincent Rouzé

# Critical, Digital and Social Media Studies

## Series Editor: Christian Fuchs

The peer-reviewed book series edited by Christian Fuchs publishes books that critically study the role of the internet and digital and social media in society. Titles analyse how power structures, digital capitalism, ideology and social struggles shape and are shaped by digital and social media. They use and develop critical theory discussing the political relevance and implications of studied topics. The series is a theoretical forum for internet and social media research for books using methods and theories that challenge digital positivism; it also seeks to explore digital media ethics grounded in critical social theorics and philosophy.

## Editorial Board



## Published

**Critical Theory of Communication: New Readings of Lukács, Adorno, Marcuse, Honneth and Habermas in the Age of the Internet**
*Christian Fuchs*
https://doi.org/10.16997/book1

**Knowledge in the Age of Digital Capitalism: An Introduction to Cognitive Materialism**
*Mariano Zukerfeld*
https://doi.org/10.16997/book3

**Politicizing Digital Space: Theory, the Internet, and Renewing Democracy**
*Trevor Garrison Smith*
https://doi.org/10.16997/book5

**Capital, State, Empire: The New American Way of Digital Warfare**
*Scott Timcke*
https://doi.org/10.16997/book6

**The Spectacle 2.0: Reading Debord in the Context of Digital Capitalism**
Edited by *Marco Briziarelli* and *Emiliana Armano*
https://doi.org/10.16997/book11

**The Big Data Agenda: Data Ethics and Critical Data Studies**
*Annika Richterich*
https://doi.org/10.16997/book14

**Social Capital Online: Alienation and Accumulation**
*Kane X. Faucher*
https://doi.org/10.16997/book16

**The Propaganda Model Today: Filtering Perception and Awareness**
Edited by *Joan Pedro-Carañana, Daniel Broudy and Jeffery Klaehn*
https://doi.org/10.16997/book27

**Critical Theory and Authoritarian Populism**
Edited by *Jeremiah Morelock*
https://doi.org/10.16997/book30

**Peer to Peer: The Commons Manifesto**
Michel Bauwens, Vasilis Kostakis, and Alex Pazaitis
https://doi.org/10.16997/book33

**Bubbles and Machines: Gender, Information and Financial Crises**
Micky Lee
https://doi.org/10.16997/book34

# Cultural Crowdfunding: Platform Capitalism, Labour and Globalization

### Edited by
### Vincent Rouzé

University of Westminster Press
www.uwestminsterpress.co.uk

Published by
University of Westminster Press
115 New Cavendish Street
London W1W 6UW
www.uwestminsterpress.co.uk

Text © The Editor and the several contributors 2019
First published 2019

Cover design: www.ketchup-productions.co.uk
Series cover concept: Mina Bach (minabach.co.uk)
Printed and bound by CPI Group (UK) Ltd, Croydon, CR0 4YY
Print and digital versions typeset by Siliconchips Services Ltd.

ISBN (Paperback): 978–1-912656-38-7
ISBN (PDF): 978–1-912656-39-4
ISBN (EPUB): 978–1-912656-40-0
ISBN (Kindle): 978–1-912656-41-7

DOI: https://doi.org/10.16997/book38



The full text of this book has been peer-reviewed to ensure high academic standards. For full review policies, see: http://www.uwestminsterpress.co.uk/site/publish. Competing interests: The authors have no competing interests to declare.

Suggested citation:
Rouzé, V. 2019 (ed). *Cultural Crowdfunding: Platform Capitalism, Labour and Globalization*
London: University of Westminster Press.
DOI: https://doi.org/10.16997/book38 License: CC-BY-NC-ND 4.0

To read the free, open access version of this book
online, visit https://doi.org/10.16997/book38
or scan this QR code with your mobile device 

# Contents

# CHAPTER 1

# Introduction

## Vincent Rouzé

### Participation in Words

The early years of the twenty-first century saw the emergence of the idea of a 'collaborative' web, a Web 2.0 where Internet users would actively participate in producing content and creating value from it. Following the financial crises and especially the dotcom crash, the term 'Web 2.0' was coined in 2005 by the American entrepreneur and expert Tim O'Reilly, with a view to rebuilding confidence among investors in the Internet (Fuchs 2008). O'Reilly was one of the first to popularize the idea that the Internet would now be based on a participative model in which the user would go from being a mere consumer to a 'content generator' (Le Deuff 2007). An identical vision was implicit in the notion of 'social media', which became common currency in the same period, despite its vagueness. In line with these different discursive propositions, specialized technical and economic apparatuses or *dispositifs*[1] for extracting value from communication flows on the web began to emerge: search engines, blogging platforms, content aggregators, virtual worlds, platforms for broadcasting video, social networks, and so on. Distinctive to these platforms is their heavy dependence on the contributions of their own user communities.

The discourses underpinning the participative and/or collaborative aspect of the Internet, along with their 'implementations', all seem to come back to the idea that pooling together the efforts of individuals can open up a better future,

**How to cite this book chapter:**

Rouzé, V. 2019. Introduction. In: Rouzé, V. (ed.) *Cultural Crowdfunding: Platform Capitalism, Labour and Globalization.* Pp. 1–13. London: University of Westminster Press. DOI: https://doi.org/10.16997/book38.a. License: CC-BY-NC-ND 4.0

one of greater solidarity and equality. The preferred tool for this is the Internet and, more broadly, digital technologies as a whole, through platforms for information exchange, and especially for crowdsourcing (i.e. collectively producing and analyzing data), crowdfunding, and providing services (like Uber and Airbnb). One can see that the principles of innovation, revolution, communities, action, and networking—are all very much present in digital discourses. It is at somewhat paradoxical to observe elements of these discourses actually suggesting a correspondence between their usages of the terms participation or collaboration and the communist project itself, that of 'an association, in which the free development of each is the condition for the free development of all' (Marx and Engels 2008: 62).

Looking past apparent points of overlap with Marx, a paradox indeed comes into view: Does the discursive rhetoric of 'empowerment' and participation, and the new services provided, really bring about individual liberation? Or are these new forms of alienation, serving a 'neo-' capitalism whose power resides precisely in mythification, in Roland Barthes's (1972) sense, and in the naturalization of everyday actions which may be simplified by digital technologies, but which are also subject to new forms of control?

## Toward Financial Participation: Cultural Crowdfunding

These questions formed the starting point of the present book, which is dedicated more precisely to studying and analyzing cultural crowdfunding platforms within a complex economic context, marked by heterogeneity and inequalities within the different cultural sub-sectors, and among their various players (Towse 2011). Such platforms have proliferated since the end of the 2000s—both those which use donation or crowdgiving models, financing projects in a disinterested, philanthropic way, and those which use reward-based models, offering different tiers of 'rewards' depending on the amount given. The best known include Indiegogo (US), Kickstarter (US), Kiva (US), Pledge-Music (UK), Artistshare (US), Patreon (US), Ulule (France), KissKissBankBank (France), Goteo (Spain), Slicethepie (UK), and Crowdculture (Sweden). These platforms' work essentially involves connecting many agents, either simultaneously or one after the other: Internet users and platform users (consumers, broadcasters, or direct backers), creative workers, traditional players in the cultural industries and neighbouring sectors (brands, sponsors, advertisers), public or para-public institutions, charitable organizations, and NGOs.

Cultural crowdfunding platforms provide truly experimental terrain for building new infrastructures, developing business models, increasing knowledge of the motivations of participating users, and establishing regimes of participation. As such, their models mainly based on gifts, with or without reward, have been extended into numerous other economic and financial sectors.

Today, they can be divided into four different models (crowdgiving, reward-based, equity, and lending), which have received the backing of international legal institutions—in France, the Banque de Prêt et d'Investissement (BPI) and the Ministry for the Economy and Finance[2]. Distinctions between these models are less a matter of thematic differences than of the different ways in which they structure economic exchanges.

In the cultural sector, donation-based and donation/reward-based platforms are the most common. The first allow philanthropist, altruistic funding of projects. Widely used for musical, literary, film and video-game projects, donation/reward-based platforms offer graduated perks according to the amount contributed. However, in Western countries, with the support of favourable legal and political frameworks, it is above all equity and lending platforms that have brought crowdfunding into the market economy. Lending-based platforms allow Internet users to lend money to third parties. As in mainstream banking, the return will depend on interest rates. Equity-based platforms enable users to invest in a project or business by becoming a shareholder and receiving dividends. These two models, which are regulated by financial market institutions and subject to the appropriate legislative frameworks, aim to let citizens and 'partners' invest in startups or projects with larger budgets. Given the potential for growth these models offer, their extension into domains other than the cultural sector indeed seems to offer a promising answer to recent financial crises and low investor confidence. These platforms have particularly attracted the attention of economic and political institutions because they generate much higher rates of return and growth than (giving- and reward-based) cultural platforms.[3] Moreover, they can prove useful in allowing businesses to bypass traditional sources of funding (business angels, banks, or venture capital funds) (Kleemann , Voß, and Rieder 2008; Lambert and Schwienbacher 2010).

Since 2012, there has been consistent growth in these platforms and the funding they raise. According to the Banque Public d'Investissement France, between 2015 and 2016 growth in France was 40%, with 21,375 projects backed and a total of €233.8m raised.[4] Figures given by the KPMG/Crowdfunding France Barometer show that, in France, crowdfunding in all its forms grew from €167 million raised in 2015 to €336 million in 2017. According to the Massolution annual report[5], worldwide growth was distributed unequally across geographical zones, with North America, Europe, and Asia at the forefront (North America $17.2 billion, Asia $10.54 billion, Europe $6.48 billion, Oceania $68.6 million, South America $85.74 million, Africa $24.16 million).

Aside from economic considerations, crowdfunding platforms have raised the hopes of a great many citizens with social, cultural, and economic projects, who see these platforms as a possible means of funding. The platforms themselves have carefully used the media to communicate their success stories. In France, for example, the crowdfunding campaign for the film *Noob*, a spinoff of the web series of the same name, received €681,046 on Ulule, having asked for

€35,000, and the roleplaying game *L'Appel de Cthulhu* received €402,985, having asked for only €10,000. New records keep on coming. In 2012, the American singer Amanda Palmer raised $1,192,793 on Kickstarter and had herself photographed with a billboard reading 'This is the future of music', calling for all artists to follow her lead. This led to an invitation to give a TED talk to promote 'The Art of Asking'.[6] We could list yet more successes that would lead us to believe that the future of funding for cultural and social initiatives lies in these forms of exchange between artists and their audiences, or between citizens. Unfortunately, as we shall see, not all projects have such a happy ending, and many fail to raise the amount they seek.

## A New Paradigm for Production and Cultural Value?

This book is therefore situated at the centre of debates over potential shifts in the production, promotion and financing of culture. Is reliance on these platforms, and the corresponding use of social networks[7], really something entirely new which has been made possible by the collaborative web? Blurring the lines between producers, consumers, and financial backers, these platforms see themselves as instruments of 'liberation' and 'value-sharing' (Lemoine 2014) which try to bring about technological and socio-economic innovation (Kuppuswamy and Bayus 2013). But do these mechanisms of monetized fundraising and exchange enable the promotion of marginal projects otherwise side-tracked by the cultural and creative industries (Cassella and D'Amato 2014; Bannerman 2012)? We might also ask whether, as suggested in the work of Boyer et al. (2016: 6), crowdfunding really participates in 'the spirit of sharing and permanent innovation', and whether it constitutes a true 'alternative' to existing financial institutions (banks, equity, business angels, and other venture capitalists)—or whether it instead heralds the emergence of new intermediaries in the cultural and creative industries (Matthews 2017).

More broadly, we want to ask how far these platforms are 'opportunities' (Kirzner 1973) for the emergence of new forms of 'creative' liberation and emancipation, and new forms of disintermediation for creative work (Bubendorff 2014). Are we seeing a democratization and diversification of cultural contents? Or do these systems just reinforce internationalized industrial logics under the cover of 'empowering' users and citizens (Bouquillon and Matthews 2010; Matthews, Rouzé and Vachet 2014)? Finally, following suggestions by Daren C. Brabham (2013: 39), we wish to consider the attitude of state and local authorities, who may see these modes of funding as an opportunity to disengage themselves, leaving the financing of culture and heritage solely in the hands of citizen-backers.

As illustrated by the work already cited, there is a vast literature on crowdfunding. It generates more interest today than research on crowdsourcing, which was dominant until the end of the 2000s. Hundreds of articles have been written on the subject. But this academic literature gives only incomplete responses to the questions set out above. This is because researchers have not taken an equivalent interest in the cultural and sociopolitical dimension, in issues surrounding the democratization of creative work, and in the politics and ethics of crowdfunding—although this final point is addressed by Scott (2015). They have tended to focus more on the platforms themselves, the way they work, and the moral and strategic added value that they contribute. This existing literature can be classified into at least three categories.

The first, which is most prominent in economics-related disciplines, management sciences, and marketing, sees crowdfunding as a potential alternative means for citizens and businesses to fund projects. Numerous works use mathematical models from microeconomics to analyze various players' interests in using crowdfunding (Belleflamme et al. 2014). Such strategic and economic (Belleflamme et al. 2015) interests are also present in articles that emphasize the importance for companies of integrating crowdfunding as a specific tool within company strategy (Bessière and Stephany 2014; Berg Grell et al. 2015). In fact, crowdfunding makes it possible to outsource tasks and to reduce the need for fundraising and investment. However, according to Belleflamme et al. (2012), nonprofit organizations are more successful at raising funds than for-profit companies: a smaller interest in profitability supposedly increases the chance of a successful campaign. Lambert and Schweinbacher (2010) make the same observation but give a different possible explanation: within the crowdfunding framework, companies are more inclined to concentrate on the quality of their product or service rather than seeking profit. Another contribution by Belleflamme et al. (2014) focuses on crowdfunding as a pre-sales system, demonstrating the emergence of a threshold beyond which crowdfunding becomes less viable than classical financing with a single investor. They also show the importance of the benefits generated through 'community building' during crowdfunding campaigns. These benefits (whose value is above all 'informational' and 'communicational') can be seen as a way to validate original ideas with a specially targeted audience.

The second category of literature, which we will mention only briefly here, is concerned with problems of national and international legislation stemming from the extension of crowdfunding to all economic sectors. In the United States, Barack Obama's 2012 Jobs Act provided for regulated financial exchanges through these platforms, and also allowed them to extend their activities—for example, by offering equity or investment in companies (Cunningham 2012). Since 2013, numerous European countries have also adopted legislation aimed both at regulating these funding methods and allowing their potential expansion to other economic sectors (Dushnitsky et al. 2016).

The third category of literature focuses on understanding the motivations of project creators and backers. For a number of scholars (Gerber and Hui 2013; Yang, Bhattacharya and Jiang 2014; Choy and Schlagwein 2016; Ryu and Kim 2016), motivations are analyzed according to models developed by behaviourist psychology, such as the work of Ryan and Deci (2000). These last identify intrinsic motivations (pertaining to the individual) and show that motivations vary from one person to another according to specific contexts (extrinsic motivations). References to this approach in research on crowdfunding aim to show what entices people to take part and contribute financially, in order to optimise campaigns and indicate what strategies should be pursued by project carriers. The work of Ethan Mollick (2015) uses econometric methods to analyze the practices of project creators on Kickstarter, and the factors involved in their success or failure. Interestingly, he notes the importance of signals about the quality and preparedness of the project and its creators: teaser videos, updates on the progress of the project, the size of the team and their presence on digital networks—all of which involve implementing 'signalling' strategies. He also notes a positive correlation between the creative output of a geographical area and the success of a campaign. This importance of geography can also be seen in the significant territorial differences in the number of projects proposed and funded, in variations in the themes proposed, and in motivations associated with proximity (Agrawal et al. 2010; Le Béchec et al. 2017).

This territorial question is also important in heritage conservation, where citizens are more likely to become engaged in and support local projects (Guesmi et al. 2015). Other studies that have looked at the motivations that drive Internet users to participate in and back projects also demonstrate the importance of affective and identity-based ties, and of supporting a cause which matches one's own values (Ordanini et al. 2011; Gerber and Hui 2013). Giudici et al. (2013) extend this work, concentrating on the factors that determine the probability of a project's success. They concentrate on the social capital of project creators, distinguishing their 'individual' social capital (which is exclusive and is measured by their presence on social networks) from their 'territorial' social capital (distributed locally, and measured by their geographical proximity to contributors). Their results suggest that individual social capital has a significant positive effect on the likelihood of achieving fundraising goals, whereas geolocalized (territorial) capital does not. In fact, the latter can act to the detriment of the crowdfunding campaign, for it marginally weakens the effects of 'signalling' in relation to individual social capital. They nevertheless indicate that, in favourable local conditions, good quality projects can easily raise funds without recourse to these platforms.


## Plan of the Book

The present volume takes up a number of questions raised in the aforementioned literature. But it is distinct both in terms of the resources it draws on and the ways in which it approaches crowdfunding platforms. Looking beyond their functions and their functional logic, and past questions of success and optimizing participation, it takes a critical socio-economic approach to the study of cultural crowdfunding platforms. Our hypothesis is that the development of these platforms, and the discourses that accompany them, are indicative of a capitalist ideology marked by the logics of 'ecosystems', of 'project-based' value creation, and of an outsourcing of tasks, which attempt to conceal the forms of labour and the social and financial apparatuses driving them. Beyond the different models represented by crowdfunding platforms, the ecosystem they claim to be a part of and the economic relations in which they are embedded are characterized by systematic outsourcing of tasks. They therefore fall under the paradigm of what Vincent Mosco (2016) calls the 'new Internet'. Along with the 'cloud' and 'big data', which denote intensified logics of control and surveillance, crowdfunding platforms confirm the transfer of value production to external entities.

Reinforcing the ideology of the 'creative project worker', entrepreneur of her/his own project, these platforms are directly and indirectly complicit in driving a reconfiguration of labour. Economic liberalization and globalization tend to absorb what were once 'alternative' experiments. This observation dovetails with the analysis of Boltanski and Chiapello (2018) who, in the second edition of *The New Spirit of Capitalism*, conveyed the importance of another city, the project-based city. Governed by the proliferation of projects, by activity rather than labour, by the need to make connections, this city displaces the orders of judgement and size. In this city, quality and size are judged in light of one's flexibility, skill set, activity, and autonomy—in other words, one's employability. As a result, the distinction between private life and professional life ceases to exist.

In line with these analyses, crowdfunding platforms contribute toward a managerial reorganization of the social world. In fact, beyond 'creativity', the 'innovation ecosystem', and the 'experiences' they propose, it does indeed seem to us that such platforms involve 'not just technical activity, but also imply social engineering [...]. The logics at work in the different platforms have been designed, and this work of design is a political gesture' (Rieder 2010: 51).

To clarify this debate, the book consists of the introduction followed by chapters 2, 3, 4 and 5, and a conclusion. Each chapter offers a distinct but complementary analysis of these questions. In the second chapter, we situate these platforms in their historical context. Vincent Rouzé shows that, far from being new, these phenomena have their roots in far older practices which they bring up to date with the use of digital technologies—fundraising, *iquib* and *tontines* are all examples of the existence of such practices before and without digital technology. He traces the ideological foundations of the participation and collaboration underlying these platforms, showing that debates about the ideas of crowdsourcing and crowdfunding typically operate with a 'managerial' conception of participation.

In the third chapter, Rouzé approaches crowdfunding through the question of the 'alternative'. The alternative may be promised by this sort of apparatus, or it may be more directly defined by these platforms' work, where the expression 'alternative finance market' is used. In either case, we should question this potential alternative, and its 'disruptive' character—in terms of the logics of intermediation involved, the partnerships forged by crowdfunding platforms, and the competing economic logics they establish. Rouzé shows how, far from being 'alternative', these platforms are new intermediaries in this creative 'ecosystem', which effectively reinforce the tried and tested logics and strategies of the capitalist cultural industry.

In the fourth chapter, Jacob Matthews and Vincent Rouzé address crowdfunding from the perspective of labour—even though the ideology of digital technologies seeks to emphasize the ludic nature of the phenomenon and leaves aside the issue of labour, both inside and on these platforms. This chapter doesn't consider project creators and platform employees separately: its original contribution is to question their activity conjointly, as both participating in the same logic of 'polymorphic entrepreneurship'.

In the fifth chapter, Jacob Matthews, Stéphane Constantini and Alix Bénistant question the role played by crowdfunding platforms in processes of globalization. The preceding chapters offer an overview and critical analysis of the platforms and their models in Western countries, but what about the Global South? Can we locate original endogenous models of crowdfunding in these regions, or do we simply encounter exogenous models that reinforce Western capitalist logics?

## Research Context

All the chapters in this book are the result of research carried out within the framework of the Collab research project, financed by the French National Research Agency (ANR) and directed by Vincent Rouzé (2015–18). Quantitative and qualitative data produced and compiled within this programme informs each chapter. As a part of this research program, we carried out fieldwork with numerous players connected to these platforms in France, in Europe (UK, Benelux, Spain), and in various countries in the Global South (sub-Saharan Africa and Latin America). Bringing together qualitative data collected as part of the ANR Collab and FDLEC[8] research programmess, the corpus is made up of more than 80 qualitative interviews with these players and with project creators in Europe (20), Ethiopia (8), South Africa (8), Senegal (9), Burkina Faso (5), Colombia (4), Brazil (16), Mexico (7), and Argentina (7).

We also use data collected through questionnaires, based on a representative sample of the population. The beta phase of the questionnaire was administered in three languages (English, Spanish and French) and received 260 responses in French (from countries including Tunisia, Senegal and Canada) and around 50 in English and Spanish. Owing to concerns about the representativeness of the sample, and faced with difficulties related to mode of administration, we limited our initial processing to the French responses. On the basis of this beta phase, we were able to develop a questionnaire centred on a solely French representative sample. This was self-administered online (over the Internet using the CAWI method). The final sample was made up of responses then categorised into three groups totalling 1,182 in all. These responses were from people aged between 18 and 66 residing in metropolitan France, from all socio-professional categories. The sample breaks down as follows:

Group 1: 312 people who had created a crowdfunding project (regardless of the project)—that is, 312 people who had already raised funds (or tried to) for one or more projects.

Group 2: 446 people who had already made pledges to crowdfunding projects (regardless of the project and the amount pledged)—that is, 446 persons who had already contributed to the funding of one or more projects.

Group 3: 424 persons who had never pledged to or created a crowdfunding project, including 194 persons who had never heard of crowdfunding, and 230 who had heard of crowdfunding but had never taken part in it.

The data collected from these participants made it possible to carry out a quantitative analysis of the practices of project creators and of donors/backers, as well as the third category of players mentioned above. This was done in order to better understand the practices that take place on and through these platforms, upstream and downstream of specific fundraising campaigns. Moreover, the qualitative data collected allowed us to study the organization of 'internal' and 'external' labour around these platforms, and the logics of cultural homogenization and transnational normalization involved in their use.

## Notes

1 Throughout this volume the term *dispositif,* translated in English by 'apparatus', is used in accordance with the notion theorized by Giorgio Agamben (2009). Broadening Michel Foucault's earlier definition, Agamben envisages it as 'that which has the capacity to capture, guide, determine, control and implement the gestures, conducts, opinions and discourses of living beings.' (p. 14).

2 https://www.economie.gouv.fr/entreprizas/crowdfunding-comment-se-lancer, accessed 8 March 2018.

3 See the following reports: *Crowdfunding Good Causes,* NESTA (2016), *Moving Mainstream: The European Alternative Finance Benchmarking Report* (2015) or the EU Commission working document *Crowdfunding in the EU Capital Markets Union,* available online at https://ec.europa.eu/info/system/files/crowdfunding-report-03052016_en.pdf

4 http://www.bpifrance.fr/A-la-une/Dossiers/Crowdfunding-un-marche-en-plein-essor/Le-marche-du-crowdfunding-francais-en-2016–34460, accessed 10 March 2018.

5 Massolution's annual crowdfunding industry report, 2015.

[6] https://www.ted.com/talks/amanda_palmer_the_art_of_asking?language= us accessed 10 March 2018

[7] Dating back to 1954 when John A. Barnes was the first to use it—well before the inception of services now commonly defined as 'social networks' (Facebook, Twitter, Linkedin, etc.)—this notion has since been adopted and adapted by a number of disciplinary fields (Mercklé 2011).

[8] 'Fondations, discours et limites de l'économie collaborative', research programme co-funded by the universities of Paris 8 and Leicester (2015–17) led by Athina Karatzogianni and Jacob Matthews.

# References

Agamben, Giorgio. 2009. *What is an Apparatus?*, trans. by David Kishik and Stefan Pedatella. Redwood City, CA: Stanford University Press.

Agrawal, Ajay, Christian Catalini and Avi Goldfarb. 2010. The Geography of Crowdfunding, NET Institute Working Paper No. 10–08.

Bannerman, Sara. 2012. Crowdfunding Culture, *Wi: Journal of Mobile Culture*, 6.4.

Barthes, Roland. 1972. *Mythologies*, trans. by Annette Lavers. New York: Farrar, Straus & Giroux.

Belleflamme, Paul, Nessrine Omrani, and Martin Peitz M. 2015. The Economics of Crowdfunding Platforms, *Information Economics and Policy*, vol. 33, p. 11–28.

Berg Grell, Kevin, Dan Marom, and Richard Swart. 2015. *Crowdfunding: The Corporate Era*. London: Elliott & Thompson.

Bessière, Véronique, and Eric Stephany. 2014. Le financement par crowdfunding: quelles spécificités pour l'évaluation des entreprises?, *Revue française de gestion*, 242.5, 149–61, <https://www.cairn.info/revue-francaise-de-gestion-2014-5-page-149.htm> [accessed 27 February 2019].

Boltanski, Luc, and Eve Chiapello. 2018. *The New Spirit of Capitalism*, 2nd edn., trans. by Gregory Elliott. London: Verso.

Bouquillion, Phillipe, and Jacob T. Matthews. 2010. *Le Web collaboratif: mutations des industries de la culture et de la communication*. Grenoble: Presses Universitaires de Grenoble.

Boyer, Karine, Alain Chevalier, Jean-Yves Léger, and Aurélie Sannajust, *Le Crowdfunding*. Paris: La Découverte, 2016.

Brabham, Daren C. 2013. *Crowdsourcing*. Cambridge, MA: MIT Press.

Bubendorff, Sandrine. 2014. Le Crowdfunding, dispositif de désintermédiation du processus de création? Expériences et discours des artistes, *Les Enjeux de l'information et de la communication*, 15.2a, 21–30 <https://lesenjeux.univ-grenoble-alpes.fr/2014-supplementA/02-Bubendorff/02-2014A-Bubendorff_pdf.pdf> [accessed 27 February 2019].

Burkett, Edan. 2011. A Crowdfunding Exemption? Online Investment Crowd-funding and U.S. Securities Regulation, *Transactions: The Tennessee Journal of Business Law*, 13.

Cassella, Milena, and Francesco D'Amato. 2014. Crowdfunding Music: The Value of Social Networks and Social Capital in Participatory Music Production in Victor Sarafian and Rosie Findley (eds.), *Civilizations 13: The State of the Music Industry/L'État de l'industrie musicale*. Toulouse: Presses de l'Université Toulouse 1 Capitole, 93–122.

Choy, Katherine, and Daniel Schlagwein (2016). Crowdsourcing for a Better World: On the Relation between IT Affordances and Donor Motivations in Charitable Crowdfunding. *Information Technology & People*, (29)1, 221–247.

Cunningham, William Michael. 2012. The Jobs Act, in *The Jobs Act: Crowdfunding for Small Businesses and Startups*. Berkeley, CA: Apress, 3–20.

Dushnitsky, Gary, Massimiliana Guerini, Evila Piva, and Cristina Rossi-Lamastra. 2016. Crowdfunding in Europe: Determinants of Platform Creation Across Countries, *California Management Review*, 58(2), 44–71.

Florida, Richard. 2014. *The Rise of the Creative Class—Revisited:* Revised and Expanded. New York: Basic Books.

Fuchs, Christian. 2008. *Internet and Society: Social Theory in the Information Age*. New York: Routledge.

Geiger, David, Stefan Seedorf, Thimo Schulze, Robert C. Nickerson, and Martin Schader. 2011. Managing the Crowd: Towards a Taxonomy of Crowdsourcing Processes, *AMCIS 2011 Proceedings—All Submissions*, paper 430.

Gerber, Elizabeth M., and Julie Hui. 2013. Crowdfunding: Motivations and Deterrents for Participation *ACM Transactions on Computer-Human Interaction (TOCHI)*, 20 (6), 1-32.

Giudici, Giancarlo, Massimiliano Guerini and Cristina Rossi-Lamastra. 2013. Why Crowdfunding Projects Can Succeed: The Role of Proponents' Individual and Territorial Social Capital, <https://ssrn.com/abstract=2255944> [accessed 27 February 2019].

Guesmi, Samy, Julie Delfosse, Laurence Lemoine, and Nicolas Oliveri. 2015. Crowdfunding et préservation du patrimoine culturel, *Revue française de gestion*, 5.258, 89–103.

Kirzner, Israel M. 1973. *Competition and Entrepreneurship*. Chicago, IL: University of Chicago Press.

Kleemann, Frank, G. Günter Voß, and Kerstin Rieder. 2008. Un(der)paid Innovators: The Commercial Utilization of Consumer Work through Crowdsourcing, *Science, Technology & Innovation Studies*, 4(1).

Kuppuswamy, Venkat, and B.L. Bayus. 2013. Crowdfunding Creative Ideas: The Dynamics of Project Backers in Kickstarter, *Social Science Research Network*, <https://papers.ssrn.com/sol3/papers.cfm?abstract_id=2234765 http://business.illinois.edu/ba/seminars/2013/Spring/bayus_paper.pdf> [accessed 27 February 2019].

Lambert, Thomas, and Armin Schwienbacher. 2010. An Empirical Analysis of Crowdfunding, *Social Science Research Network*, <http://ssrn.com/abstract=1578175> [accessed 27 February 2019].

Le Béchec, Marriannig, Sylvain Dejean, Camille Alloing, and Jérôme Meric. 2017. Le Crowdfunding des projets culturels et ses petits mondes, <https://halshs.archives-ouvertes.fr/halshs-01508423/> [accessed 27 February 2019].

Le Deuff, Olivier. 2007. Le Succès du Web 2.0: histoire, techniques et controverse, <https://archivesic.ccsd.cnrs.fr/sic_00133571/document> [accessed 27 February 2019].

Lefèvre, Fantine, and Bogdan Filip Popescu. 2015. *Le Crowdfunding à la française*. Paris: Presse des Mines.

Lemoine, Phillipe. 2014. La Nouvelle Grammaire du succès: la transformation numérique de l'économie française. Report to the French Government.

Liu, Yang P., Prasanta Bhattacharya, and Zhenhui Jiang. (2014). *Video-Evoked Perspective Taking on CrowdFunding Platforms: Impacts on Contribution Behavior*. Auckland: ICIS.

Marx, Karl, and Friedrich Engels. 2008. *The Communist Manifesto*. London: Pluto.

Matthews, Jacob T. 2017. Beyond 'Collaborative Economy' Discourse: Present, Past and Potential of Digital Intermediation Platforms, in James Graham (ed.), *Collaborative Production in the Creative Industries*. London: University of Westminster Press, 33–50. DOI: doi.org/10.16997/book4.c

———, Vincent Rouzé and Jérémy Vachet. 2014. La culture par les foules, in *Le Crowdfunding et le crowdsourcing en question*. Paris: MKF Éditions.

Menger, Pierre-Michel. 2002. *Portrait de l'artiste en travailleur: métamorphoses du capitalisme*. Paris: Le Seuil.

Mercklé, Pierre. 2011. *La sociologie des réseaux sociaux*. Paris: La Découverte.

Mollick, Ethan R. 2015 Delivery Rates on Kickstarter, *Social Science Research Network*, <http://papers.ssrn.com/abstract=2699251> [accessed 27 February 2019].

———, and Nanda Ramana. 2015. Wisdom or Madness? Comparing Crowds with Expert Evaluation in Funding the Arts, *Social Science Research Network*, <http://papers.ssrn.com/abstract=2443114> [accessed 27 February 2019].

Mosco, Vincent. 2016. Après l'Internet: le *cloud*, les *big data* et l'internet des objets, *Les Enjeux de l'information et de la communication*, 18, 253–264. <https://www.cairn.info/revue-les-enjeux-de-l-information-et-de-la-communication-2016–2-page-253.htm> [accessed 27 February 2019].

NESTA. 2016. *Crowdfunding Good Causes: Opportunities and Challenges for Charities, Community Groups and Social Entrepreneurs*. Available at https://media.nesta.org.uk/documents/crowdfunding_good_causes-2016.pdf

Ordanini, Andrea, Lucia Miceli, Marta Pizzetti, and Ananthanarayanan Parasuraman. 2011. Crowd-funding: Transforming Customers into Investors

Through Innovative Service Platforms, *Journal of Service Management*, 22(4), 430–470.

Rieder, Bernhard. 2010. De la Communauté à l'écume: quels concepts de sociabilité pour le 'Web Social'? *tic&société*, 4.1, <http://journals.openedition.org/ticetsociete/822> [accessed 27 February 2019].

Ryan, Richard M. and Edward L. Deci. 2000. Intrinsic and Extrinsic Motivations: Classic Definitions and New Directions, *Contemporary Educational Psychology*, 25 (1), 54–67.

Ryu, Sunghan and Young-Gul Kim. 2016. A Typology of Crowdfunding Sponsors: Birds of a Feather Flock Together?. *Electronic Commerce Research and Applications*, vol. 16, 43–54

Scholz, Trebor (ed.). 2012. *Digital Labor: The Internet as Playground and Factory*. London and New York: Routledge.

Scott, Suzanne. 2015. The Moral Economy of Crowdfunding and the Transformative Capacity of Fan-ancing, *New Media & Society*, 17(2) 167–182.

Stegmaier, Jamey. 2015. *A Crowdfunder's Strategy Guide: Build a Better Business by Building Community*. Oakland, CA: Berrett-Koehler.

Towse, Ruth. (ed.). 2011. *A Handbook of Cultural Economics*. (Cheltenham: Edward Elgar).

# CHAPTER 2

# Crowdsourcing and Crowdfunding: The Origins of a New System?

## Vincent Rouzé

The main purpose of this chapter is to examine the supposedly innovative nature of crowdfunding. We will illustrate how ancient practices, whether widely recognized or consigned to history, have been recuperated by players in the digital world in order to surpass or update them through 'innovation', but also to legitimate their own practices and stimulate a movement dependent upon 'creative' users, or even a 'creative class' (Florida 2014). The chapter will therefore address and challenge crowdfunding's self-declared 'revolutionary' character—the claim that it necessarily represents the future of the financing of culture, since it rests upon collaborative and collective forms of creation, mutual assistance, financing, and participation.

In reference to the work of Michel Foucault, what interests us here is a first attempt at an 'archaeology' of crowdfunding. Foucault emphasizes that archaeology is a 'systematic description of a discourse-object' (Foucault 1972: 156) which, rather than reducing observed contradictions, instead focuses on the history of ideas, multiplying discontinuities and describing 'the different *spaces of dissension*' (Foucault 1972: 170). He adds that archaeology is the 'interaction of rules that, in a culture, determine the appearance and disappearance of statements, their persistence or their disappearance, their paradoxical existence as *events* and *things*' (Foucault 2014: 708). The issue here, then, is to understand

---

**How to cite this book chapter:**

Rouzé, V. 2019. Crowdsourcing and Crowdfunding: The Origins of a New System?. In: Rouzé, V. (ed.) *Cultural Crowdfunding: Platform Capitalism, Labour and Globalization*. Pp. 15–33. London: University of Westminster Press. DOI: https://doi.org/10.16997/book38.b. License: CC-BY-NC-ND 4.0

how current platforms have been constructed on multiple ideological grounds, all of them fertile, and how they are marked by 'object-discourses' that serve 'reconfigured' capitalist logics. For it is clear that the only new thing about crowdfunding is its name. Its participative and financial logics existed long before digital technologies and the Internet.

The first part of this chapter seeks to define the neologisms 'crowdsourcing' and 'crowdfunding'. This is a subject of debate between those who argue that crowdfunding should be seen as a particular type of crowdsourcing, and others who believe it to be something separate. In the second part, we examine the 'revolutionary' label often applied to these platforms, showing that, if anything, this refers in fact to the 'permanent revolution' proper to capitalism. We then situate the question of crowdfunding in continuity with a certain ideology of the Internet, and show that the origins of the logic of gift and counter-gift are pre-digital. We then question the logic of gift–counter-gift at work in the majority of cultural crowdfunding platforms, and conclude by examining the managerial and competition-led nature of these platforms. Far from generating truly revolutionary practices, they transform participation into an operational tool in the service of more traditional economic aspirations, ones that do nothing to reduce inequality.

## Crowdsourcing, Crowdfunding: One and the Same Thing?

To understand crowdfunding's ideological basis, we must trace the word's semantic genealogy. Today, crowdfunding often occupies a significant place in the discourse of political, economic, cultural, social, and even citizen players. But it rests on a broader concept, from which it emerged: crowdsourcing.

This neologism designates a set of activities on the part of Internet users (design, production, expertise, valuation, promotion, broadcast, distribution) on specialized web platforms. Basing his own work on that of James Surowiecki (2004)—who defends the idea of the 'wisdom of crowds' and the need to develop 'collective intelligence', endorsed by the researcher Pierre Levy in the late 1990s—the American journalist Jeff Howe (2006) has, strangely, become an academic reference for understanding the phenomenon. Howe gives a useful definition of crowdsourcing:

> Simply defined, crowdsourcing represents the act of a company or institution taking a function once performed by employees and outsourcing it to an undefined (and generally large) network of people in the form of an open call. This can take the form of peer-production (when the job is performed collaboratively), but is also often undertaken by sole individuals. The crucial prerequisite is the use of the open call format and the wide network of potential labourers (Howe 2006).

Through a number of examples (including Amazon's Mechanical Turk, Inno-Centive, iStockphoto), he observes that new strategies are developing which rely on communities to produce content, resolve problems and 'innovate' through the work of a large number of participating Internet users, who are willingly described as a 'crowd'.

This contemporary resurgence of the term 'crowd' tends to make each of its supposed members' singularities invisible, and to gloss over socio-economic inequality. The fear expressed in early mass media studies of a supposed dissolution of the individual into unstable collectives, each with its own logic, each adding up to more than the sum of their parts, finds its counterpart in Surowiecki's bestselling *The Wisdom of Crowds*. Surowiecki argues that aggregating the information circulating between a weakly cohering set of individuals can yield results (in terms of cognition, coordination and cooperation) that are broadly superior to the performance of any individual member of the group. He writes that, 'in the right circumstances, groups are remarkably intelligent, and are often smarter than the smartest people in them' (Surowiecki 2004: xiii). This implicitly recognizes the importance of systems that allow the activities of these collectives of physically isolated individuals to be harnessed and stimulated. It recognizes, in short, that crowdsourcing and crowdfunding platforms are indeed *dispositifs*[1] or apparatuses for the mobilization of economic players (of labour and of capital). In the article cited above, Howe adds that crowdsourcing should therefore be defined as the outsourcing of tasks to a large number of persons in view of constructing a project or resolving a problem, but from a strategic and economic perspective.

The issue is to put out a call for projects broad enough for a majority of 'workers' to take part. The term 'work' or 'labour' is all-important here, since the appeal is not made by a community, but on the initiative of businesses and/or institutions. As Howe explains in *Crowdsourcing: A Definition* (2006), crowdsourcing therefore cannot be compared to the Harvard economist Yochai Benkler's concept of 'commons-based peer production', characterized by a decentralized collective production that is network-based, modular and open to all. The socio-economic model developed by Benkler (2006) is based on collective and collaborative production by individuals. From this point of view, hierarchical logics seem to disappear in favour of horizontal decision-making. Unlike in capitalist economic strategies, financial compensation and return on investment are either disregarded or relegated to secondary concerns.

Frank Kleemann, Günter Voß and Kerstin Rieder reinforce this opposition: 'The essence of *crowdsourcing* is the intentional mobilization of creative ideas and other forms of labour for commercial exploitation' (Kleemann, Voß and Rieder 2008: 22). The researcher Daren C. Brabham adds that crowdsourcing is 'a hybrid model that blends the transparent and democratizing elements of open source into a feasible model for doing profitable business, all facilitated through the web' (Brabham 2008: 82).

This phenomenon is primarily analyzed in terms of 'efficiency', involving the relations between the tasks to be accomplished, the populations concerned and the returns (Corney et al. 2009; Geiger et al. 2011). It is overwhelmingly viewed in terms of productivity (Huberman, Romero and Wu 2009) or 'open innovation'. Corney et al. (2009) propose that crowdsourcing can be defined in terms of three dimensions. Firstly, they categorize crowdsourcing depending on the nature of the tasks (for instance, creation, value creation, or organization). They then outline a second dimension related to requirements (what individual, collective and expert skills are needed). The third dimension concerns the sort of remuneration offered (whether the work will be voluntary or paid, for instance). The French researchers Schenk and Guittard (2011) use a concept of crowdsourcing which encompasses the conclusions of earlier work, setting their argument in a managerial framework. Doan, Ramakrishnan and Halevy (2011) approach the problematic of crowdsourcing systems on the web from a broader perspective: as well as classifying the nature of the tasks and players that define the system, they also discuss the implicit or explicit nature of the collaborative labour, and its impact on the objectives to be achieved. The net outcome is a multiplication of activities, and dozens of potential definitions of crowdsourcing. According to the Spanish researchers Estellés-Arolas and González-Ladrón-de-Guevara (2012) there are at least thirty-six original definitions, ranging across all disciplines.

This means the term can be applied indistinctly to multiple activities, digital or not. The label has become an 'umbrella' term (Geiger et al. 2011; Ridge 2014), an 'all-encompassing' and 'generic' label (Belleflamme et al. 2011: 3). This often renders it 'inoperative' or, from the opposite point of view, makes it flexible enough to apply to multiple activities that are difficult to distinguish or define. In our quantitative study of a sample of French Internet users, only 9% were capable of giving a definition of crowdsourcing and citing specific platforms and projects.

Nonetheless, in many respects these definitions intersect with the concept of convergence developed by the American researcher Henry Jenkins (2006). On the basis of his early research on fans, Jenkins suggests that participative culture marks a point of meeting and convergence between industrial and media strategies, on the one hand, and user-produced content on the other. With the same emphasis on 'empowerment' and collective intelligence, Jenkins sees this as enabling a transformation of traditional industrial logic. From that point on, the 'ascendant innovation' championed by researchers like Von Hippel (2005), and the 'anointing' and 'cult' of the amateur described by the French researcher Patrice Flichy (2010), were seen as emancipatory for individual and collective alike. A majority of works and articles follow this common theme of a 'positivist' return of the amateur, concentrating on the development of new digital usages, horizontal relations modifying the production and capitalisation cycle and increased cultural democratization. However, some critical assessments stand out, such as the work of former Silicon Valley entrepreneur Andrew Keen

(2007) or that of digital media pioneer Jaron Lanier (2011), who both note new forms of alienation and subjection. For proponents of the 'positivist' position it is 'natural' (in Roland Barthes' mythological sense of naturalization) that this turn toward the Internet user/citizen should be accompanied by a financial commitment, allowing them to realize the projects they are most passionate about.

Crowdfunding thus becomes the financial offshoot of crowdsourcing (Rouzé, Matthews and Vachet 2014; Lebraty and Lobre-Lebraty 2015) The aim is not just to invite 'amateurs' to produce content, but more generally to encourage them to offer financial backing to whatever they are passionate about, supporting projects run by their friends or which they believe in (a phenomenon sometimes called 'love money'). In this way, the financial aspect of the arrangement disappears, and the participative, affective and experiential dimension takes centre stage.

But other researchers claim that, while crowdfunding may be descended from crowdsourcing, it is a distinct phenomenon. According to Belleflamme, Lambert and Schweinbacher (2014), its primary aim is to optimize the flow of information between manufacturers and consumers, particularly by allowing the collection of consumer data, so that crowdfunding platforms can serve as tools for evaluating the quality of goods and services for prospective consumers. Ultimately, they see such platforms as promotional and marketing tools in both business-to-business and business-to-consumer markets: Crowdfunding can be seen as a concept that goes beyond simple fundraising: it is a way of developing industrial activities through the process of financing (Belleflamme, Lambert and Schweinbacher 2014: 586). For others, the difference between crowdfunding and crowdsourcing is related to collaboration: in crowdsourcing, participants influence content; in crowdfunding, they never do.

This brief etymological and epistemic detour allows us to discern the main issues related to crowdfunding platforms. First of all, the protean logic of crowdsourcing is answered by the segmented logic of crowdfunding, as well as the importance of logics of outsourcing and gearing responses to a strategic demand produced by the greatest number. Far from the logic of the 'commons' the term initially flirted with, most players think of crowdfunding in terms of efficiency and the experience of the citizen/social actor. This paves the way for the development of its financial aspect, which combines the outsourcing of content production with the outsourcing of modes of financing, the reduction of risk on the part of consumers/investors, and the development of devolved modes of labour.


## Crowdfunding: A Revolution?

Given the above definitions, it is intriguing how often crowdfunding is described as revolutionary. In 2013, the French website Mediapart published an article titled 'What Is Crowdfunding and Why is it Revolutionary?'[2] In the same year, a book appeared with the title *The Crowdfunding Revolution: Social Networking Meets Venture Financing* (Lawton and Marom 2013). A few years later, an article in *Forbes* declared that 'Santander Joins the Crowdfunding Revolution.'[3]

Is the financing of projects by supposedly numerous and unknown donors, in a horizontal community-based fashion, really revolutionary? If we look at the dictionary definition of 'revolutionary', applying it to crowdfunding platforms implies that they 'overturn established principles; transform modes of thinking and action and procedures of fabrication' by allowing collaboration and forms of horizontal participation. The use of the term is not neutral. In the case of crowdfunding, it refers to a wider conception. Texts such as those of CerPHI (Centre d'Étude et de Recherche sur la Philanthropie) [Cazemajou] 2013), with evocative titles like 'Crowdfunding as an Innovative Technology for Financing and Promoting Business Projects', emphasize the revolutionary character of these platforms:

> It can be argued that crowdfunding [is] an innovative financial service; the main idea is based on cooperation in the form of the collective funding of different kinds of projects to achieve set objectives, implemented through capital formation, which comes in small amounts from a large not previously known number of people on the basis of open competition using Internet technologies. (Hryhoruk and Prystupa 2017)

Berg Grell, Marom and Swart (2015) add that we must embrace this revolutionary character by integrating crowdfunding as a new instrument, whether internal or external, in the service of businesses—an instrument that promotes cohesion, team spirit and competition.

The revolutionary dimension of crowdfunding, then, seems to rest upon the innovative nature of the way in which it generates collective cooperation to finance projects on the basis of open competition. This tells us everything we need to know. All of these terms illustrate the necessity of a 'permanent revolution.'[4] But this is not the revolution of the emancipation of the people and the proletariat, reinventing themselves on an egalitarian basis, which Marx and Engels, and later indeed Trotsky proposed, rather, it is that of capitalist exploitation, an economic, 'open', 'innovative', 'competitive' revolution which occurs in a context of cyclical crises.

## Crowdfunding: An Old Story Reinvented

As we have seen, discourses about crowdsourcing and crowdfunding both conceptualize and facilitate the creation of economic models that transform existing relations between the sphere of production and that of consumption[5], formerly organized on a 'top-down' model. This strategic recuperation of horizontal models of action, creation and sharing is legitimated through references to historical forms, which the players of crowdfunding attach themselves to and rely upon. Two mutually reinforcing stories of crowdfunding are told: one about ideology, described above, which is based on the history of a collaborative Internet; and one that identifies it with older practices like fundraising. Whatever the references and examples used, this historicization of the phenomenon raises challenges for the various players involved. It seeks to secure the legitimacy of these practices through their naturalization, but also and above all to promote the 'pioneering' contribution and 'innovative' character of these digital platforms.

### *1. A History Legitimated by the Internet*

In an article that proposes a 'brief history of crowdfunding', the American researchers David Freedman and Matthew Nutting (2015) situate the birth of the crowdfunding system in the US, prior to the emergence of the aforementioned dedicated platforms. They argue that the phenomenon emerged in 2004 on the platform Artistshare with the jazz musician Maria Schneider. Following a call for backers via this platform, Schneider succeeded in raising $130,000 to produce a new album, which won a Grammy Award in 2005. Crowdfunding was born in the music sector—so often a pioneer in the metamorphosis of the so-called 'creative' industries. Kappel (2009) documents the many initiatives in operation, dividing them into two financing models (the 'betting model' and the 'investing model'). Slicethepie (UK) finances bands and musicians on the betting model. Sellaband.com (UK) and Bandstock.com (the Netherlands), both founded in 2006, instead developed the 'investment' approach, and are the forerunners of today's crowdfunding platforms.

We might situate the birth of crowdfunding even earlier, with the innovative initiative of British prog-rock band Marillion, who in 1997 launched a pre-sale of their album on their website, successfully raising $60,000 to finance a US tour.

Other researchers, including Flannery (2006), locate the birth of crowdfunding in 2006, with the website Kiva. Following Maguire (2013), the French management science researchers Méric, Jardat, Mairesse and Brabet (2016) note that the first use of the term 'crowdfunding' goes back to August 2006, on the blog of Michael Sullivan, in reference to his project 'Fundavlog': 'Many things are important factors, but funding from the "crowd" is the base on which all else depends on and is built on. So, crowdfunding is an accurate term to help me explain this core element of Fundavlog'.

In tracing the history of crowdfunding by way of the Internet, the aim is to place it in the ideological lineage of the free and participative, DIY nature of its precursors. This involved a mobilization of the community in the service of furthering knowledge, and a common culture proper to the Internet (open source movements, the first bulletin board systems, and more broadly speaking the alternative technology movements that appeared over the course of the 1970s).

And yet this genealogy is only partial. These pioneers of information technology were seeking a way of sharing and collaborating based on equal, non-competitive and non-economic exchange. This opposition becomes very visible in debates and legal action concerning piracy, where two opposing visions of the Internet are set against each other.

Numerous studies (Flichy 2007; Cardon 2010; Castells 2001; Fuchs 2008) describe how the emergence of the Internet was the complex result of an encounter between 'many circles' (Cardon 2010) and 'many cultures' (Castells 2001)[6], mostly hailing from universities and groups of amateur technology enthusiasts or hackers. In his article 'Where the Counterculture Met the New Economy', Fred Turner shows that, alongside innovations by those working in research institutions, the disparate activist groups that emerged directly from the alternative movements of the 1960s and 1970s played a considerable role in the early experiments that led to the development of modern digital communications networks. With none of the desire for control characteristic of the mainstream culture and media industries, these users designed and developed communications systems according to their own needs and personal aspirations, and as a function of the communities they belonged to. The creation of new protocols for exchanging data normalized communications between members of these communities. For example, it was this process that led to the gradual adoption of the standard for email address formatting designed by Ray Tomlinson in 1971, which would lead to the development of email as we now know it.

The main idea guiding the development of these networks (which were not yet interconnected) was collaboration, and the sharing of data—software, algorithms and programming languages—which allowed users to contribute to the development of this nascent world. These networks were structured according to a deliberately decentralized schema.

As the sociologist Philippe Breton has shown (1992), the 'meritocratic and collective' ideology which drove hackers and academics borrowed heavily from the 'cybernetic utopia' of the physicist and mathematician Norbert Wiener, with its 'unbridled circulation' of information. 'Free software' emerged at the beginning of the 1980s with the GNU project and the creation of the Free Software Foundation, led by the programmer Richard Stallman. It incontestably represented a concrete incarnation of this combination of decentralization and collaboration.

Far removed from any concerns about financial remuneration, intellectual property, or contractualization, the idea of free software was dependent on source code that was open and could be freely altered, modified and improved. This led to a decentralized conception of knowledge, visible in Wikipedia, the first collaborative online encyclopedia project. The hacker logic functioned on the model of a gift economy: one gives to the community (a software package, an improvement, a text), and can expect reciprocation (Castells 2001: 63). As a result, legitimacy in the community was established independently of its members' initial socio-economic position.

Participative and communitarian logic is certainly at the heart of these first, emblematic cases of collaborative financing and production mentioned above and, in large part, it also marked the broadening out from these first virtuous circles towards other amateur users. Yet it should be emphasized that—setting aside their subsequent expansion—these initial practices did not rely on denouncing capitalist economics and society, any more than they saw themselves as part of an opposition to them.

As Turner (2005) has shown, it is above all a matter of the productions of groups and individuals who, having temporarily 'retired' from the dominant ways of life (joining neo-rural communities in the 1970s), returned to urban centres over the course of the following decade, and there invented new 'life-styles' in which information technology practices seemed an asset in terms of both cultural and economic capital. These digital 'pioneers' combined economic neoliberalism and libertarian political convictions, something that may seem surprising from a European, and especially a French point of view. But this was a non-negligible ingredient in the fertility of the Bay Area for IT start-ups (Barbrook and Cameron 1996). From the mid-1990s onward—particularly after Congress rescinded the ban on online commerce (Flichy 2007)—these collaborative uses of the web were increasingly resolutely embedded within a 'new economy' concerned above all with profitability (even if rational valuation was no longer a priority), and which was increasingly coveted both by institutional investors and by oligopolistic players from the culture and communications industries.

### 2. A History Legitimated by Pre-Digital Collaborative Cultural Financing and Production

The other way in which crowdfunding is legitimated involves situating it in a more distant past, locating its origins in participative funding, whether in terms of simple gift-giving, or a logic of gift-giving and rewards. These models have come in many forms and formats, and have gone by many names, including patronage, *tontine* and fundraising. Their main shared feature is fundraising for projects using collective mobilization and participation.

Religions, for example, have long used this as a major expansion strategy. In the name of 'charity' and 'saving souls', or by imposing taxes, financial and/or material participation on the part of the community (for instance, through bequests and donations) has financed artistic work, the construction of hundreds of monuments, and aid to the poor. This and many other historical examples could be developed further, but such a question obviously exceeds the scope of this volume. Therefore we have selected just a few examples specifically involving cultural financing.

The emergence of a market for books in Europe in the sixteenth century makes for an interesting starting point. Beginning in this period, two methods of financing emerge which have clearly collaborative elements. Firstly, publishing associations and cooperatives were established, where individuals came together in the form of a mutual fund to share the financial risk associated with printing and distribution, as well as potential profits. This system was more prominent in the French market, but over the course of the following centuries it progressively spread across much of political and activist publishing. Secondly, the same period saw the development of publication by subscription, a model initiated in England in the seventeenth century, and an obvious forerunner of the modern cultural crowdfunding model. The publisher made a prospectus which presented the work, and this was distributed to potential buyers, who could then subscribe to buy a copy and would have their names printed among the list of funders inside the book. Publication depended on the number of subscribers and, in particularly successful cases, the amount raised made it possible to reprint the book for what we would now call the 'traditional' market.

We must keep in mind that, at the time, this method of financing through 'mutualist cooperation' was not seen as a marginal model, or as a last resort. Instead, we should think of it as one of many coexisting forms of capitalization during this period—one which, in some cases, was distinctive for entirely short-circuiting the professional figure of the expert, evaluative editor still familiar to us now. For example, this system was used to publish most of Jane Austen's novels, with certain aristocratic subscribers paying a higher price before publication and having their name printed in the finished book. This model also met with great success in the US, even up to the end of the nineteenth century. Mark Twain's books were initially published exclusively in this way, as the curators of an exhibition at Cornell University Library on Twain note:

> The subscription publication industry blossomed in post-Civil War America. Tens of thousands of sales agents, many of them veterans and war widows, canvassed small towns and rural areas armed with a sales prospectus and a 'book' containing sample pages and illustrations, and offering multiple binding options to fit every décor and price range. Prospective buyers selected a binding and signed an agreement to pay for the book when it was delivered to their door. (CLU 2010)[7]

This is a model very close to that of those gift–counter-gift platforms that offer different tiers of reward depending on the amount given.

Closer to our own times, let us consider the emblematic case of the independent film *Shadows*, by John Cassavetes, which came out in the US in 1959. The British critic Thomas Jarvis describes the conditions under which it was made:

> To retain artistic autonomy Cassavetes had to be creative in raising money and finding equipment for the film. He arranged an interview on Jean Shepherd's *Night People* radio show, and told the DJ about the improvisation and the idea for the movie. When asked how he was going to fund the film, Cassavetes replied; 'if people really want to see a movie about people they should just contribute the money'. After that radio listeners started mailing in money to the station. For the next two years Shepherd would keep listeners up to date with the making of *Shadows*, which he described as 'their film'.[8]

The example is interesting in two respects. It clearly illustrates the continuity of a phenomenon which, from Beethoven's *Missa Solemnis* to the vast number of 'alternative' projects on platforms like Rockethub and KissKissBankBank, promote crowdfunding as a (more or less successful) attempt to escape the apparatuses of economic, political and ideological domination. And the call for financial contributions which Cassavetes made on the late-night radio show played a part in the emergence of specialized media (specialized by age category, subcultural group and so on—something that reaches all the way to today's virtual communities). In this respect, it incarnates one of the modern myths cultural crowdfunding and crowdsourcing depend on: that of the media's capacity to 'translate between the language of professionals and the desires of the public' (Hennion 1993: 305). Jean Shepherd described *Shadows* to her audience, her users, as being 'their' film—a reference to 'their' decision to finance its production. One must also note the importance of similar modes of funding in the field of politics and the press. The French communist newspaper *L'Humanité* has regularly relied on public subscriptions in order to maintain its daily publication, and permanent fundraising has been similarly used by FM radio stations in North America as an alternative or a complement to advertising revenue. These are clearly not novel phenomena, as one might also consider the case of the Bolshevik newspaper Pravda, which was set up by Lenin in 1912 and relied then on a network of 40 000 regular reader/donators (Elwood 1972).

Finally, current approaches to crowdfunding are linked to problematics about heritage preservation. The financing of the Statue of Liberty in New York is often cited as an argument that crowdfunding was not born with the Internet. As Pitts (2010) says, 'the pedestal for the Statue of Liberty was funded in 1884 by Joseph Pulitzer through an open call to the American people and funded through micro-donations'. In fact, numerous funding 'campaigns' were needed before the project was completed. Note also that, anticipating methods which are now commonplace on crowdfunding platforms, the French designer Bartholdi exhibited various already finished pieces (the arm holding the flame, for example), and organized a lottery offering mostly art-related gifts (Moreno 2000).

Beyond these Western practices, we should also note that collective financing for social and cultural projects exists in many other countries in different forms and under various names. Community fundraising campaigns in Africa, called *umgulelo* in Xhosa, have traditionally been held in the form of fixed and regular contributions, under the authority of groups of community leaders who are responsible for sharing out the money to those in need, for funerals and marriages, building houses, and starting businesses. These modalities of gift in Africa and among diasporas also occur in *tontines*—a word derived from the name of the Italian banker Lorenzo Tonti, who in the seventeenth century advised Cardinal Mazarin to use this type of financing. They come in real estate, financial and associative forms, all of which consist in giving a sum on a regular or one-time basis to help fund individual or collective projects in the community.

The forerunners of what we now call cultural crowdsourcing and crowdfunding are many and various, from subscriptions to more or less limited oppositional modes of production, via talent shows and reality TV music shows as fictional representations of ideal collaborative production. However, this does not imply the abandonment of alternatives (in the primary sense) for certain types of content, or in particular economic, cultural, geographical or ideological contexts.

## The Logic of Gift–Counter-Gift in Question

It is true that the first crowdfunding platforms were based on the gift. But above all they were based on the gift–counter-gift model. Once again, we must ask whether these ancestral models of exchange just translate existing models into digital form, or whether they have been updated for the digital age and the Internet.

The question of the gift is at the core of the work of French anthropologist Marcel Mauss (2001), who studied Amerindian societies. As Florence Weber suggests in her introduction (2007) to the republication of Mauss's book, many researchers remember only potlatch, an agonistic struggle for prestige, which might lead them to see the logic of gift and counter-gift as a permanent struggle. But this ignores the fact that the same logic is at work in another form: Kula. First studied by Bronisław Malinowski (*Argonauts of the Western Pacific*, 1922 [2002]), Kula involves a peaceful ceremonial exchange, rather than one marked by conflict and the possibility of establishing a social hierarchy in the community.

We may hypothesize that this logic of the gift is objectively at work in many cases of crowdsourcing, where users produce and share content without financial considerations entering into the matter directly. Obvious instances of this can be found in literature, including the wiki-novel project *A Million Penguins*, initiated by the British publishing house Penguin, which received 11,000 contributions. Such examples come in different forms, involving both authors and readers in interactive games which often end up blurring the boundaries between them. These forms of creation and their subsequent promotion involve not only literature, but also education and information. Following the logic of gift and counter-gift, each participant is alternately creator and user, producer and consumer, regardless of their real social status and legitimacy. As in the primitive societies Mauss studied, only these activities contribute to the construction of the community and the status which each person has within it. Wikipedia is equally emblematic of this. And, while the names of the initial creator and the contributors remain, they are no longer of primary importance. Contributors' names disappear in favour of the content produced, at the same time as the distinction between author and reader, or musician and listener, disappears—with all the associated dangers for the veracity and diversity of the content on offer (Kittu and Kraut 2008).

But this logic is far less certain in the case of crowdfunding. The problematic of gift and counter-gift is prominent once more, but in a very different form to that highlighted by Mauss. The name and figure of the project's creator play a fundamental role in crowdfunding platforms, providing a way of managing and/or creating a sense of proximity. Here, the gift is above all financial. Only the counter-gift recalls the original nature of the principle, since it is given by project creators in the form of 'rewards' allocated according to the amount pledged. Depending on the platform, this remuneration may, for example, come in the form of a free concert, a copy of the album with a dedication (for a musical project), or numbered prints (in the case of photography projects). These cases are more like forms of pre-purchase (Kappel 2009).

The issue for these platforms is to offer an original experience embedded within an economic approach, integrating the process within industrial strategies that ultimately lead to acts of consumption (whether anticipated or not). The processes of intermediation we explore in the next chapter link together creators, platforms and industrial players (from cultural or other sectors). They also make it possible to limit the financial risk inherent to cultural production, while allowing for a better match between the personalized, segmented demands of consumers and the potential diversity offered by creators. Creation and participation can be integrated into industrial strategies in the name of shared experience and registers of 'attention'. The notion of experience here therefore also refers, implicitly, to an experiment (*expérience*) in the scientific sense: provoking a specific phenomenon in order to observe it and draw a set of rules—a 'systematic logic', as Husserl calls it. Such observation led to the establishment of the first platforms with cultural aims, whose purpose was to comprehend the system and extend it to other economic sectors. In this sense, the experiential/experimental logics of collaborative financing and production, the research on motivation cited in the introduction, and algorithms and data, all contribute to the emergence of new strategies of control which we examine further in chapter 3.

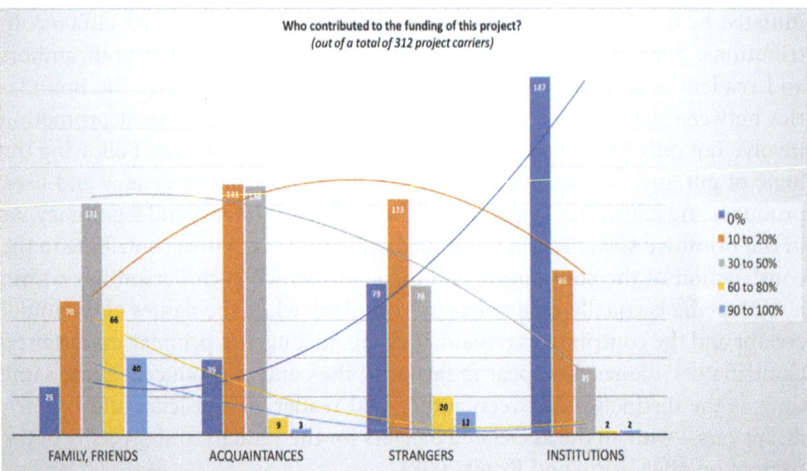


**Figure 1:** Source: ANR Collab 2017.

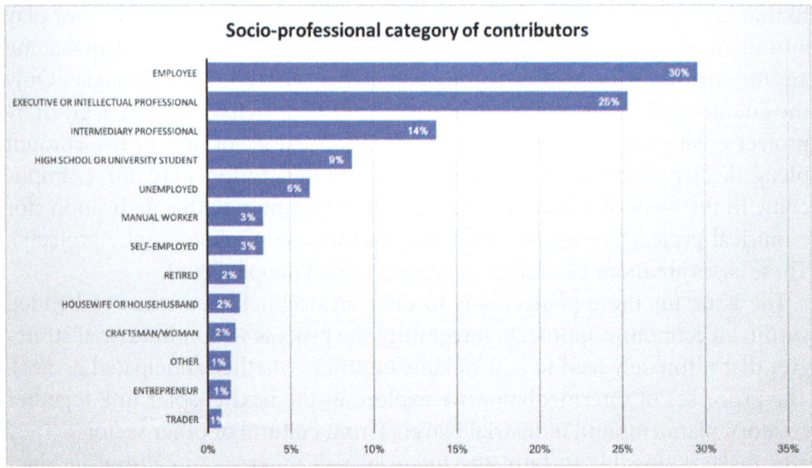


**Figure 2:** Source: ANR Collab 2017.

## Conclusion

The revolution under discussion involves not so much the various modes of gift-giving as the modes of reaching a larger audience, to which the homogenizing and extremely contestable label of the 'crowd' is applied; and with altering social organization by making (productive and financial) participation into an original economic tool. As we have seen, the quest for collective financing is nothing new, but with the Internet it opens up a larger space, 'the crowd', and becomes integrated into capitalist logics aimed at innovation and open competition. In this context, the term 'crowd'—widely criticized in the social sciences and in research on media reception—has been reborn. We are far from Gustave Le Bon's 'crowd psychology' (1926 [1895]), which depicted crowds as indistinct, irrational entities which were dangerous to his own bourgeois vision of society. The modern use of the term implies that the Internet allows one to reach a 'crowd' of people. The shortcomings of this globalizing, homogenizing conception of social groups brings to mind the analyses put forward by Raymond Williams in the conclusion of his work *Culture and Society*, regarding the shift of focus from 'crowds' to 'masses'; Willians rightly points out that this semantic shift is ideologically motivated: 'the term has been capitalised for the purposes of political or cultural exploitation' (Williams 1960: 319). Not only do these terms attempt to provoke fears and conceal social struggles and inequalities; Williams also asserts: 'There are in fact no masses; there are only ways of seeing people as masses' (Ibid.). This comment is just as valid in the case of 'crowds'.

Interestingly, the reference to 'crowds' has been erased in French legislative texts. The *Journal Officiel* (which publishes all official national laws and decrees) validated the translation of crowdfunding by '*financement participatif*' (participative funding), hence hinting at more individualised usages but keeping with a sense of homogenization. The Quebec French usage of the term 'sociofinancement' (social funding) is also worth noting. These forms avoid any reference to both communities (or indeed communitarianism), and to the remanence of social inequality. As shown by our quantitative research, launching a project on a crowdfunding site involves the participation of one's family, acquaintances and—something far more difficult—a number of people one does not know.

Perhaps we should end by emphasizing that, behind this participative ideology, we can glimpse a desire to extend financial participation and innovative competition everywhere and into all everyday relations, putting the collective in the service of individual goals. We also see, in line with the conclusions of Raymond Williams referred to above, an attempt to use the concept of the 'crowd' to hide social and class inequalities.

The quantitative data collected during our research (figure 2 opposite) shows that these platforms are mostly invested in and financed by so-called 'middle' and 'higher' socio-professional categories.[9] They render social stratification invisible in the name of this 'creative class'—but there is no way this can hide the inequalities in access, use, and financing that exist on these platforms.

## Notes

[1]  See endnote 1, p.9.
[2]  https://blogs.mediapart.fr/mark-white/blog/200613/what-crowdfunding-and-why-it-revolutionary Accessed 10 September 2018.

[3] https://www.forbes.com/sites/davidprosser/2016/10/05/santander-joins-the-crowdfunding-revolution/#51df71894e60 Accessed 10 September 2018.

[4] This remark can be linked to the thesis developed by American historian Joyce Appleby in her work *The Relentless Revolution: A History of Capitalism* (2010). She shows how capitalism pertains not only to the sphere of economics but exists most significantly as a cultural construction, in constant evolution, feeding off its many contradictions.

[5] This logic reminds one of the role and 'invention' of communication as a means of 'fluidifying' internationalized economic exchanges, from the 19th century onwards, as theorized by Armand Mattelart in his work *La communication-monde* (1992).

[6] Castells uses the term 'culture' here in a somewhat restrictive way, pointing to a 'shared technical universe' whose practices contribute *in fine* to creating 'different technical modes of thought' among users (2001: 58).

[7] http://rmc.library.cornell.edu/twain/exhibition/subscription. Accessed 30 March 2019.

[8] https://www.popoptiq.com/a-look-back-at-john-cassavetes-shadows-a-pioneering-movie-in-the-history-of-american-independent-cinema/. Accessed 30 March 2019.

[9] Further results of this study can be consulted on the research programme's website: https://projetcollab.wordpress.com/2018/02/05/enquete-sur-les-usages-du-crowdsourcing-et-du-crowdfunding/ Accessed March 30 2019.

## References and Reading


Appleby, Joyce. 2010. *The Relentless Revolution: A History of Capitalism*. New York: Norton.

Barbrook, Richard, and Andy Cameron. 1996. The Californian Ideology, *Science as Culture*, 6(1), 44–72.

Belleflamme, Paul, Thomas Lambert, and Armin Schwienbacher. 2014. Crowdfunding: Tapping the Right Crowd, *Journal of Business Venturing*, 29(5), 585–609.

Benkler, Yochai. 2006. *The Wealth of Networks: How Social Production Transforms Markets and Freedom*. New Haven, CT: Yale University Press.

Berg Grell, Kevin, Dan Marom, and Richard Swart. 2015. *Crowdfunding: The Corporate Era*. London: Elliott & Thompson.

Brabham, Daren C. 2008. Crowdsourcing as a Model for Problem Solving: An Introduction and Cases. *Convergence: The International Journal of Research into New Media Technologies*, 14(1), 75–90.

Breton, Phillipe. 1992. *L'Utopie de la communication: l'émergence de l'homme sans intérieur*. Paris: La Découverte.

Cardon, Dominique. 2010. *La Démocratie internet: promesses et limites*. Paris: Seuil.

Castells, Manuel. (2001). *The Internet Galaxy: Reflections on the Internet, Business and Society.* Oxford: Oxford University Press

Castells, Manuel. 2009. *The Rise of the Network Society.* Oxford: Wiley Blackwell.

Cazemajou, Louis. 2013. *La place du crowdfunding philantropique,* CERPHI, <http://www.cerphi.org/wp-content/uploads/2013/11/La-place-du-Crowfunding-Philantropique.V22.pdf> [accessed 27 February 2019].

Corney, Jonathan R., Carmen Torres-Sánchez, A. Prasanna Jagadeesan, and William C. Regli. 2009. Outsourcing Labour to the Cloud, *International Journal of Innovation and Sustainable Development*, 4(4), 294–313.

Doan, AnHai, Raghu Ramakrishnan, and A.Y. Halevy. 2011. Crowdsourcing Systems on the World-Wide Web, *Communications of the ACM*, 54(4), 86–96.

Elwood, Ralph Carter. 1972. Lenin and *Pravda*, 1912–1914, *Slavic Review*, 31(2): 355–380.

Estellés-Arolas, Enrique and Fernando González-Ladrón-de-Guevara. Towards an Integrated Crowdsourcing Definition. 2012. *Journal of Information Science*, 38(2), 189–200

Flannery, Matt. 2006. Kiva and the Birth of Person-to-Person Microfinance, *Innovations*, 2(1–2), 31–56.

Flichy, Patrice. 2007. *The Internet Imaginaire'*, trans. by Liz Carey-Libbrecht. Cambridge, MA: MIT Press.

———. 2010. *Le Sacre de l'amateur: sociologie des passions ordinaires à l'ère numérique.* Paris: Seuil.

Florida, Richard. 2014. *The Rise of the Creative Class—Revisited: Revised and expanded.* New York: Basic Books.

Foucault, Michel. 1972. *The Archaeology of Knowledge*, trans. by A.M. Sheridan Smith. New York: Pantheon.

———. 2014. *Dits et écrits (1980–1988)*, vol. 3. Paris: Gallimard.

Freedman, David M., and Matthew R. Nutting. 2015. *A Brief History of Crowdfunding Including Rewards, Donation, Debt, and Equity Platforms in the USA.* <http://www.freedman-chicago.com/ec4i/History-of-Crowdfunding.pdf> [accessed 27 February 2019].

Fuchs, Christian. 2008, *Internet and Society: Social Theory in the Information Age.* New York: Routledge.

Geiger, David, Stefan Seedorf, Thimo Schulze, Robert C. Nickerson, and Martin Schader. 2011. Managing the Crowd: Towards a Taxonomy of Crowdsourcing Processes, *AMCIS 2011 Proceedings—All Submissions*, paper 430.

Hemer, Joachim. 2011. A Snapshot on Crowdfunding, Working Papers Firms and Region, No. R2/2011, <http://hdl.handle.net/10419/52302> [accessed 27 February 2019].

Hennion, Antoine. 1993. *La Passion musicale: une sociologie des mediations.* Paris: Métailié.

Howe, Jeff. 2006. Crowdsourcing: A Definition, Crowdsourcing blog, https://crowdsourcing.typepad.com/cs/2006/06/crowdsourcing_a.html [accessed 5 March 2019].

Hryhoruk, Pavlo, and Lyudmila Prystupa. 2017. *Crowdfunding as an Innovative Technology for Financing and Promoting Business Projects*. Available at: http://elar.khnu.km.ua/jspui/bitstream/123456789/6371/3/Coll_mon_IER_2017_print_vol_3-135–143.pdf> [accessed 27 February 2019].

Huberman, Bernardo A., Daniel M. Romero, and Fang Wu. 2009. Crowdsourcing, Attention and Productivity, *Journal of Information Science*, 35.6, 758–765.

Jenkins, Henry. 2006. *Convergence Culture: Where Old and New Media Collide*. New York: New York University Press.

Kappel, Tim. 2009. Ex Ante Crowdfunding and the Recording Industry: A Model for the U.S.?, *Loyola of Los Angeles Entertainment Law Review*, 29(3), 375–85.

Keen, Andrew. 2011. T*he Cult of the Amateur: How Blogs, MySpace, YouTube and the Rest of Today's User-Generated Media Are Killing Our Culture and Economy*. London: Hachette UK.

Kittur, Aniket, and Robert E. Kraut. 2008. Harnessing the Wisdom of Crowds in Wikipedia: Quality through Coordination, in *Proceedings of the 2008 ACM Conference on Computer Supported Cooperative Work*, 37–46.

Kleemann, Frank, G. Günter Voß and Kerstin Rieder. 2008. Un(der)paid Innovators: The Commercial Utilization of Consumer Work through Crowdsourcing, *Science, Technology & Innovation Studies*, 4(1), 5–26.

Lanier, Jaron. 2010. *You Are Not a Gadget: A Manifesto*. New York: Vintage

Lawton, Kevin, and Dan Marom. 2013. *The Crowdfunding Revolution: How to Raise Venture Capital Using Social Media*. New York: McGraw-Hill.

Le Bon, Gustave. 1926 [1895]. *The Crowd: A Study in Popular Mind*. London: T. Fisher Unwin.

Lebraty, Jean-Fabrice, and Katia Lobre. 2015. *Crowdsourcing: porté par le foule*. London: ISTE Editions.

Maguire, Anna. 2013. *Crowdfund It!* Braddon: Editia.

Malinowski , Bronisław. 1922 [2002]. *The Argonauts of the Western Pacific*. Abingdon: Routledge.

Mattelart, Armand, 1991. *La Communication-monde*. Paris: La Découverte.

Mauss, Marcel. 2001. *The Gift*. Abingdon: Routledge.

Méric, Jérôme, Remi Jardat, François Mairesse, and Julienne Brabet. 2016. La Foule, *Revue française de gestion*, 5, 61–74.

Moreno, Barry. 2000. *The Statue of Liberty Encyclopedia*. New York: Simon & Schuster.

Pitts, J.B. 2010. Pulitzer Crowdfunded the Statue of Liberty? Available at: http://dailycrowdsource.com/2010/10/20/earth/geography/pulitzer-crowdfunded-the-statue-of-liberty

Rheingold, Howard. 2000. *The Virtual Community: Finding Connection in a Computerized World*. Reading, MA: Addison-Wesley Longman.

Ridge, Mia (ed.) 2014. *Crowdsourcing our Cultural Heritage*. Abingdon : Ashgate.

Rothler, David, and Karsten Wenzlaff. 2011. *Crowdfunding Schemes in Europe*. EENC Report, vol. 9.

Schenk, Eric, and Claude Guittard. 2011. Towards a Characterization of Crowdsourcing Practices, *Journal of Innovation Economics & Management*, 1, 93–107.

Surowiecki, James. 2004. *The Wisdom of Crowds*. New York: Anchor.

Turner, Fred. 2005. Where the Counterculture Met the New Economy: The WELL and the Origins of Virtual Community, *Technology and Culture*, 46(3), 485–512.

Von Hippel, Eric. 2005. *Democratizing Innovation*. Cambridge, MA: MIT Press.

Weber, Florence. 2012. The Gift: Towards an Ethnography of Non Market Services: Preface to Marcel Mauss *The Gift* 2nd edn. Paris: Presses Universitaires de France. Available at: http://www.sciences-sociales.ens.fr/IMG/file/Florence%20WEBER%20The%20Gift%202012.pdf

Williams, Raymond. 1960. *Culture and Society*. New York: Anchor Books.

# CHAPTER 3

# Far from an Alternative: Intermediation Apparatuses

## Vincent Rouzé

In the face of economic crises, increased concentration in the cultural industries and the withdrawal of public support, crowdfunding platforms seem to offer new opportunities for funding and promoting culture (D'amato 2014). In 2013, Fleur Pellerin—former French junior minister in charge of the digital economy—visited the peer-to-peer personal lending startup Prêts d'Union. In her speech, she argued that crowdfunding is 'a simple and effective alternative which allows innovative businesses to perform better, and investing citizens to support the projects of creators and talented entrepreneurs which are close to their own hearts and which resonate with their own beliefs.' Once we get beyond such seductive speeches to young entrepreneurs—made in a 'crisis' context—these integrated platforms can be viewed as stakeholders in the 'alternative finance market'.

But in what way are those platforms disruptive? Are they really alternatives, and if so, what makes them alternative? Is it their approach to project funding, which contrasts with the caution and reluctance banks and institutions typically show? Are they an alternative to corporate finance? If so, how can this alternative also apply to culture? This chapter seeks to answer these questions by analyzing how crowdfunding platforms operate and what functions they actually perform. The key hypothesis is that they constitute *dispositifs* or

**How to cite this book chapter:**
Rouzé, V. 2019. Far from an Alternative: Intermediation Apparatuses. In: Rouzé, V. (ed.)
  *Cultural Crowdfunding: Platform Capitalism, Labour and Globalization*. Pp. 35–58.
  London: University of Westminster Press. DOI: https://doi.org/10.16997/book38.c.

apparatuses (Agamben, 2007) in the economic and social realm as well as on a political and legal level. In this regard, they contribute to the implementation of what Philippe Corcuff (1998) calls 'action regimes' of a predominantly normative (rather than alternative) type. Unlike the experimental, DIY-inspired fundraising modalities of early Internet sites, mainly in the field of music, the platforms which have arisen since 2010 are inherently conceived as new intermediary players within the fragmented cultural economy.

In the first section we will discuss the polysemic nature of the concept of the 'alternative' in order to expose the ambiguities of its usage regarding the case of crowdfunding platforms. Subsequently, we will expose how the different apparatuses tend to transform these platforms into central players typically following a logic of intermediation (Miège 2017). Lastly, we will question the notion of an 'alternative' from the viewpoint of project carriers. Although they may be experienced as alternative by project creators, in reality they are better understood as new intermediaries firmly integrated within the prevalent capitalistic logics of the cultural and creative industries.

## Defining the Alternative

The notion of alternative is commonly attached to forms and systems which seek to exist and define themselves at the margins or in opposition to the existing, dominant models. From a strictly etymological point of view, the term has two key meanings. Firstly, it refers to 'that which acts in turn' (as in alternative electrical current); secondly, as of the sixteenth century, to 'that which replaces'. It is clearly the second meaning that qualifies numerous practices or systems, but this usage is complex given that it pertains to such a variety of contexts and situations. As we are reminded by John Downing's analysis on radical media, 'everything, at some point, is alternative to something else' (Downing 2001: p. ix). Nonetheless, what characterises them beyond this diversity is the specific goals which they exist for: either these practices aim to critique, transform and abolish the system within which they appear, or they seek to accompany the system's structural mutations in order to maintain its hegemony (in the Gramscian sense).

Much existing literature in the field of alternative media has shown how, in the first case, these forms aim at emancipation and wider participation, various degrees of radical transformation. According to Marisol Sandoval and Christian Fuchs (2010) these alternative, militant forms are articulated around two divergent conceptions, which they name subjective or objective, in reference to a formulation put forward by Anthony Giddens. The first defines the alternative according to the actions carried out and the location of these last. The central point is that participation generated allows expression for individuals and groups that are deprived of it in traditional media. Horizontal and collective modes of control and organisation complete this, with DIY-inspired processes leading to more democratic forms of 'management'. The second, objective, conception refers to work more concerned with contents, and with radical and critical media forms as such, envisaging these as a counter-force against existing institutions. It's this dimension that is at play in artistic and cultural forms in the fields of music (Kruse 1993), film (Newman 2009) or literature, in the sense that they strive to transcend or abolish existing codes and norms, as well as mainstream economic or political logics, despite simultaneously running the risk of being reintegrated into a capitalist system that feeds on such alternatives. The case of the punk movement, as analysed by Dick Hebdige (1979), is a classic illustration of this phenomenon. And as Christian Fuchs (2010) also observes, despite their emancipatory goals, alternative media practices and contents must also avoid three major pitfalls: the fragmentation of the public sphere; their profitability and links with repressive political purposes; their tendency towards exclusivity.

This tension between two conceptions of the alternative can be seen at play in the literature regarding propositions and alternative economic models. On the one hand one observes a number of reflections and concepts pertaining to alternatives to globalized and centralised capitalist economies, covering closely related themes and suggesting new practices such as an end to speculation, the development of alternative currencies (Greco 2001), the importance of locally based, participatory practices and non-hierarchical labour relations. On a second level, one observes critical analyses of the capitalist system, illustrating the contradictory logics which it thrives upon (Hardt and Negri 2001, Boltanski and Chiapello 2018). In both cases the aim is to rebuild solidarities based upon both material and symbolic reappropriations, forms of 'entrepreneurship of the multitude'—to quote Hardt and Negri's (2017) somewhat optimistic formula discussed also by Fuchs (2017)—marked by practices of the 'commons', open co-operation (Bauwens and Kostakis, 2014), as opposed to capitalist exploitation. They can also be set within the project a sustainable ecology (Löwy 2011) or that of 'degrowth' (Latouche 2014).

As we observed in the previous chapter, the spread of Internet extends these debates and the tension between a development based on citizen controlled, alternative, collective sites and platforms, and online spaces run according to the capitalist logics of the culture and communication industries. In these debates, a majority of so-called 'alternative' platforms are given (or seek) this appellation in opposition to the mainstream, international market leaders (Facebook, Uber, Netflix, etc.). A recent contribution to this question (Thuillas and Wiart 2019) suggests three types of 'alternative' platforms: firstly the mutualist, assembling several existing cultural players which gather to develop a common project; secondly virtual 'marketplaces' allowing various independent players to join forces in order to increase their market share; thirdly those supported by public or para-public funding. The last case, only, allows a certain degree of independence from the logic of financial returns. It can however be easily constrained by political logics favouring such and such a project, requiring legitimisation of local or national power structures. In all cases, these types of platforms are only partially concerned with the alternative logics discussed above, and appear most likely to contribute to the reinforcement of political and/or economic hegemony.

Crowdfunding platforms, in their overwhelming majority, appear to be characterised by these dominant logics. The term 'alternative', as used by the French Junior Minister in the speech quoted at the beginning of this chapter, has to be considered according to its second finality, i.e. without any explicit reference to forms of emancipation, to critical models, or to the transformation of the existing system. This usage of the term goes hand in hand with the praise of 'innovations' and 'creativity' which are specifically designed to extend capitalism's lease, so as to speak. It belongs to a somewhat hazy ideology of participation which can indeed alternately be declined to the 'gift economy', the 'collaborative economy', the 'gig economy', the 'peer economy', etc. In practice what these various notions share is the commodification of daily activities which formerly were beyond the realm of market economy, either because of their inherently private nature, or because they remained until recently publicly supported (Scholz 2016).

As with the majority of platforms and with the ideologies that accompany their usages (Gillespie 2010), cultural crowdfunding platforms can be seen as positioned on the fringes of traditional cultural-industrial logics. To ensure their financial viability, platforms apparently adopt the so-called 'long tail' model (Anderson 2006): instead of developing and securing niche markets, they secure niche projects, in a 'grey zone' of the cultural industries, led by project creators and their communities. Unlike the logic of rarity-based artistic and cultural markets (Farchy, Sagot-Duvaroux et al. 1994), these platforms offer a huge number of projects, most of which are not aimed at an audience much beyond the 'crowd' of participants/backers. This is confirmed by the presence of heterogeneous projects, and by the fact that these are largely one-offs which appear on rapid rotation (financing over periods of 2 months, less than 180 days on average), asking for an average of €4,365 (source BPI France).[1] Their alternative features rely, moreover, in the forms of financial transaction that they offer, supposedly on the margins of mainstream finance. Several titles of NESTA annual reports are, from this point of view, quite eloquent: *The Rise of Future Finance: The UK Alternative Finance Benchmarking Report* (2013); *Understanding Alternative Finance: The UK Alternative Finance Industry Report* (2014).

Crowdfunding platforms undeniably reflect some of the values and ideas that one also can find in alternative discourses and projects: participation, horizontality, the strength of local, community-based projects, the autonomy of project creators—but consistently in forms which are compatible with capitalist economic logics. These forms of participation are therefore very much removed from, or even in contradiction with, concepts such as Participatory Economics (or Parecon) developed by the American economist Robin Hahnel and writer activist Michael Albert (1991). These last proposed to wholly rethink the economy on the basis of socially shared needs and desires, both within the structures and values of labour, in a respectful relation to the environment, and in view of a social justice inspired by democratic decision-making procedures, and initiatives carried out during the twentieth century in various revolutionary contexts, from Soviet Russia to Latin America.

In other words, we can see that crowdfunding platforms are indeed apparatuses in the sense suggested by Giorgio Agamben (2009), who argued, following Michel Foucault, that the apparatus 'has in some way the capacity to capture, guide, determine, control and implement the gestures, conducts, opinions and discourses of living beings'. In the following section we will consider what precise functions these apparatuses perform.

## Apparatuses Adapted to Market Strategies

Following the diversification and segmentation of the traditional cultural industries, and integrating other economic sectors through their emphasis on creativity (Garnham 2005; Tremblay 2008), cultural crowdfunding platforms (gift and reward-based models) now operate in competitive two-sided markets (Eisenmann et al. 2006; Rochet and Tirole 2006) and must develop their appeal and their selling points in order to survive according to capitalist modalities that are not specific to the digital sector. Aiming to better understand the economics of platforms and the issues involved in them, a study by DARES (Direction de l'Animation de la Recherche, des Études et des Statistiques) emphasized that 'the economics of platforms does not constitute a radical new break; the model pursues, combines and multiplies dynamics already largely at work during the 1990s' (2017: 10).

They have indeed developed on the model of the intermediary, as an interface between different players (Miège 2017), and an instrument of industrial convergence (the 'ecosystem'). According to a report by the Conseil National du Numérique en France, a platform is:

> a service fulfilling an intermediary function for access to information, content, or services, either published or supplied by a third party. Apart from its technical interfaces, it organizes and hierarchizes content in view of its presentation and interconnection with end users. To this common characteristic is sometimes added an ecosystemic dimension characterized by interrelations between convergent services.[2]

This double movement of interface and convergence plays a part in the extension and financialization of 'amateur' practices, the outsourcing of problem solving, and content production, while reducing the risks of investment by shifting them to the user/consumer and/or community (Matthews 2015a; 2015b). Given these practices, the platforms develop a twofold discourse that reveals the ambiguity of their position. They present themselves to creators and backers as an 'alternative'; simultaneously, they position themselves as partners rather than competitors to traditional industries. Sector professionals we spoke to believe that this globalized competitive 'ecosystem' is now 'mature'. Cultural crowdfunding platforms can therefore be differentiated according to distinct strategies aimed at differentiated markets. We now set out these various modes of differentiation.[3]

### *1. Discussing the Typology of Platforms*

Let's firstly recall the dominant typology. Donation based platforms allow contributors to fund a project in a purely 'philanthropic' fashion; reward-based platforms offer graduated gratifications according to the amount given; lending based platforms invite users to lend money in exchange for expected interest returns; lastly, equity based platforms allow users to invest in a project or a company by becoming a shareholder and therefore expecting dividends. This classification is widely shared by both economic and political players and attempts to differentiate various forms of exchange or investment. Although it underlines the extension of the fields in which crowdfunding is now operating, it is nonetheless problematic. Firstly, this classification erases structural distinctions that can exist within one single category. Secondly, it fails to address the specificities of each platform. For instance, in 2018, the French professional organisation 'Financement Participatif France' listed together 22 platforms hosting cultural or 'solidarity' projects which were either donation based or reward based. Lastly, this nomenclature fails to acknowledge the development of 'internal' platforms belonging to either private corporations or public institutions. This is the case of the 'Tous Mécènes' platform developed by the famous Musée du Louvre, which therefore cannot be accounted for with the commonly recognised typology. Therefore, we propose another classification, which corresponds more clearly to the activities and specificities of the various platforms studied, particularly in the field of the communication and culture industries.

### *2. Generalist Platforms*

The first type of platforms encountered are the media-fuelled generalist sites such as Indiegogo, Kickstarter or Rockethub in the USA, or Ulule and KissKiss-BankBank in France. They allow project creators to raise funds for a variety of cultural goods or services (music, book or other printed media publishing, fiction or documentary film, videogames, as well as technological projects, apps, etc.). These platforms generally involve funding projects over a short period of time (the 'campaign'), but it is also possible for projects or persons to be funded by 'backers' over a long or undetermined period—a route offered by Patreon in the USA and Tipee in France.

The generalist platforms have the biggest turnover, and capture the majority of value in terms of both number of projects submitted and amounts raised—Indiegogo and Kickstarter in the US, Ulule and KissKissBankBank in France. Kickstarter, the world leader, has raised $4,090,777,676 across a total of 157,152 projects funded. The figures are lower in France: Ulule reports 26,261 projects funded out of 40,643 submitted, generating donations amounting to €129,564,662 since the platform's launch. KissKissBankBank raised €93,488,678, with 33,175 projects proposed, 19,349 of which were successful.

| Platforms | Number of submitted projects | Number of funded projects | Success rate % | Total amount collected by platform |
|---|---|---|---|---|
| Kickstarter (US) | 432,016 | 157,152 | 36.37 | $ 4,090,777,676 |
| Ulule (F) | 40,643 | 26,261 | 64.61 | € 129,564,662 |
| KissKissBankBank (F) | 33,175 | 19,349 | 58.32 | € 93,488,678 |

**Source:** compiled from data made public by each platform, January 2019

The dominance of generalist platforms is due both to thematic categorizations (close, if not identical, to those of the cultural and creative industries: music, comics, publishing, films and documentaries, videogames, technology, cookery), and to their media coverage and trust they generate. This observation is corroborated by the statistics of the research we carried out with Internet users, project creators and backers. To the question 'Can you cite any crowdfunding platforms?' respondents to our study mostly named Ulule (27%), KissKissBankBank (22%), Leetchi (13%) and Kickstarter (9%).

More specifically, regarding the projects submitted on the majority of platforms, music appears to account for a significant proportion of revenues. The importance of music can be explained partly by the ties that this art form has with crowdfunding from the beginning, but also because of the correspondence between musical formats, as an experience good, with this type of apparatus (Bourreau and Gensollen 2006)—unlike other areas such as documentary or fiction film, whose products both require significantly larger budgets and often rely on diverse sources of funding. Lastly, this importance can be linked to the structure of the musical sector and the evolution of usages in the digital age (Leguern 2016). For instance, considering the figures of US platform Kickstarter, in June 2019, music isn't generating the most projects but it remains the category where there are the most fully funded projects.

| Projects on Kickstarter | Number of submitted projects | Number of fully funded projects | Success rate % |
|---|---|---|---|
| Music | 59,879 | 29,707 | 49.90 |
| Film and video | 71,612 | 26,731 | 37.55 |
| Games | 45,907 | 17,652 | 38.94 |
| Publishing | 46,640 | 15,018 | 32.47 |
| Theatre | 11,907 | 7,077 | 59.94 |
| Dance | 4,129 | 2,546 | 61.86 |

Source: compiled from data made public by the platform, June 2019

In France, one observes different hierarchies according to each platform. On KissKissBankBank 5,988 musical projects were submitted, making it the most funded category with an average contribution of 54€ and a 72% success rate. On Ulule, although the musical category comes third (with 4,315 submitted projects and 16.6 million euros raised) behind social/citizenship projects and film (20.6 million; 6% and 72%). The gap between the number of projects submitted and the success rate can be explained by editorial and selective logics, as well as by the fact that some cultural categories rely on more specific and very implicated communities. As a corollary to the higher number of projects submitted, these generalist platforms attract a higher number of backers as compared to thematic and/or niche platforms (16,466,075 donors for Kickstarter, 1,665,223 'kissbankers' for KissKissBankBank). They also generate projects that bring in amounts far higher than the initially requested sum.

However, both the platforms' own figures and those of private bodies must be taken with a pinch of salt, as they are based on data that differs in terms of both space and time, making comparison difficult and perhaps impossible. Note also that only the major platforms even supply such figures. The data exhibited by these platforms serve as a communicational and promotional showcase, and testify to a demand for transparency on the part of users. But they remain difficult for the researcher to verify. This explains why we've had access to far more data from generalist platforms than regarding those which cater for a single specific artistic or cultural form.

### 3 Niche Platforms

Faced with this newly competitive market, more specific thematic and niche platforms are developing, or trying to compete, in increasingly specialised cultural sectors. These include platforms like Blue Bees (which focuses on ecological agriculture and food), Touscoprod for documentary and cinema, Sandawe for comics, the platform and label Microcultures for music, and Weezart, currently in beta form, which offers fair revenue distribution for artists. Platforms have also emerged which are specifically dedicated to sport, like Fosburit, or religion, like Credofunding. The number of submitted and funded projects are understandably much lower, as are the total amount collected, in comparison with generalist platforms.

| Platforms | Number of submitted projects | Number of funded projects | Success rate % | Total amount collected by platform |
|---|---|---|---|---|
| Sandawe | n.c | 175 | n.c | € 3,094,530 |
| Fosburit | n.c | n.c | n.c | n.c |
| Credofunding | 1,923 | 453 | 23.55 | € 4,488,147 |

**Source:** compiled from data made public by each platform, January 2019

With stricter and more assertive editorial selection, these platforms are (or try to be) rooted in particular communities. But within this competitive context, the lifespan of many is short, as was the case for the music platform Pro-8moi, Myartinvest, for buying art (now closed), or Touscoprod, which has been 'integrated' into Proarti.


### 4 Local Platforms

The third model is based upon the alternative value of locally situated initiatives and hence pertains to 'local' platforms. Since 2010 we have seen the promotion and creation of such platforms, whether general or niche. With the hope of reaching funders no longer uniquely on a family basis, local platforms have developed that are rooted in a particular region and host local projects. These include Kocoriko (Grenoble), Gwenneg (Brittany), Kengo.BZH (Brittany), J'adopteunprojet (Poitou-Charentes), and Ma Belle Tribu, started by CASDEN Banque Populaire, which aims to support 'outstanding citizen and community initiatives in the regions'. Similar initiatives are underway in Quebec through platforms such as La Ruche and Haricot.

Certain general platforms have also taken the hint, investing in local development: Ulule, for instance, now runs 'Ulule Tours' in France and Quebec. Mixing cultural and community elements in this way, with the participation of public and private institutions, only confirms what was said above in regard to partnerships. For example, in 2014, the French rail company SNCF launched a project on Ulule. With the aim of safeguarding the artistic heritage of the station at Tours, SNCF Gares et Connexions partnered with the association

| Platforms | Number of projects submitted | Number of funded projects | Success rate % | Total amount collected by platform |
|---|---|---|---|---|
| La Ruche | n.c | 175 | n.c | 3,300,277 $ Can (2,173,958 €) |
| Haricot | n.c | 400 | n.c | 1,035,356 $ Can (681,947 €) |

Source: compiled from data made public by each platform, January 2019

'Patrimoine-Environnement', inviting users to back the renovation of eighteen ceramic tile paintings by the artist Eugène Martial. They raised €10,381, having requested only €8,000. Platforms help blur the lines between public and private institutions, and between the responsibilities distinctive to each. At work here is a communications strategy: the desire to create a community of users, but also and above all to outsource to users and to citizens the costs of the renovation of properties that belong to them.

## 5 Combined Platforms

The fourth model involves a regime of private-public interrelation. On the private side, such platforms may function on the basis of public endowments,[4] for example, as is the case with Proarti, which promotes art and culture, or Dartagnans, which aims to disseminate and preserve French culture and heritage. In this case, they are supported by public initiatives ranging from certification by the Ministry of Culture to 'aid' given by regional and departmental authorities through local councils. The way in which they work varies, insofar as they can select which projects to support, can offer support to them outside of a strictly economic logic, and are thus able to consider the aesthetic dimension of the project.

## 6 Integrated Platforms

The fifth and final model is that of the platform as a tool integrated into internal entrepreneurial strategies. Following a market logic, 'corporate' platforms are now being set up to improve relations between businesses and their clients. On the model of the advertising platform Eyeka, these have now become a tool developed, managed and used in corporate strategies. Oscillating between the logics of crowdsourcing and crowdfunding, the platform becomes a tool for businesses which integrates pre-existing strategies. As Grosman and Brandes (2015) explain, using the example of IBM, 'corporate' crowdfunding enables internal collaboration and the synergising of different activities of the business and its staff, but it also enables bonding, competition and interaction between 'co-workers'.

Finally, regardless of the models developed and the strategies deployed, startup platforms have the same dependencies as the projects they help develop. Project creators depend on the investment of their community and, similarly, platforms depend on their own investors. In order to grow and develop they must carry out regular, substantial fundraising, public and private, as already analyzed in the framework of the so-called 'collaborative' web (Bouquillion and Matthews 2010). As a result there are uncertainties as to their future, but there is also growing competition, leading to the takeover and/or demise of platforms—as illustrated by the closure of MyMajorCompany in 2016.

## The 'Ecosystem' as a Stimulus for Extensive Partnerships

The third point follows from the logics of intermediation created in this way. It particularly involves the search for partnerships that will allow these platforms to be integrated into the existing economic 'ecosystem', making them new intermediaries—which somewhat tempers, while not entirely invalidating, the idea of the alternative. If the notion of the 'ecosystem' resonates with both environmental issues and the core questions posed by the 'commons' movement, it is implemented in a wholly different perspective here. The 'ecosystem' we hear so much about must be understood in terms of a double movement of synergetic partnerships and competition driven and regulated by the market economy. The new world market, made up of a myriad of small- and medium-sized economic players linked by digital communications networks, supposedly depends on the systematization of peer-to-peer approaches in the economic domain, as well as on a hypothetical fusion between the spheres of production and consumption, as described in *The World is Flat* (Friedman 2005) and *Wikinomics* (Tapscott and Williams 2006).

The partnerships forged can be of different types, sometimes private, sometimes public, and sometimes by way of white-labelling. They may change over time. In France, from its very beginning the platform MyMajorCompany was associated with the music label Warner, which handled its publishing and distribution. In 2010 it chose to diversify its activities by moving into literary publishing, and forged an alliance with the publisher XO. In 2011, wanting to enter the comics sector, it formed a partnership with the Belgian group Media Participations, owner of Dupuis, Dargaud and Le Lombard publishing houses, and in parallel it formed other partnerships with companies as diverse as the insurer AXA, the interiors store Habitat and the music streaming site Spotify. In 2018, KissKissBankBank announced partnerships with numerous public and private players, including La Banque Postale, the newspaper *Le Parisien*, a number of Chambers of Trade and Industry, and MK2 cinemas. Ulule's partnerships are less visible, and seem instead to work by inviting local companies and collectives to function as white label products, and through targeted and branded campaigns. The UK's number one cultural project platform, Crowdfunder (a spin-off of the equity platform Crowdcube) boasts numerous such partnerships with a range of companies including M&S, Santander, Virgin Business, AXA, JCDecaux), as well as universities and local authorities across the country.

In all cases, the partnerships rely on players from the traditional cultural and creative industries, on local and regional authorities, as well as on associations and charity groups, hence providing a reservoir of fresh creative labour and renewing the oligopoly/fringes model—while at the same time blurring the distinction between public and private players, which is treated as unimportant in the new 'ecosystem'. In the digital era, the principal factor in an economic player's expansion is supposedly no longer its ability to optimize transaction costs internally, but its propensity to conduct and organize transactions on an 'open market' (Tapscott and Williams 2006: 56).

Despite the 'publicizing' of these partnerships, which promotes an image of synergy and dynamism, platforms are more discreet about their ultimate goals. Referring to Gillespie (2010), Bullich (2015) says about YouTube that platforms have an interest in playing on semantic ambiguity, revealing only those aspects of their work that present them in the best light and leaving the strategic, operational and economic dimensions in the shadow. This is done to maintain an image that is neutral and sympathetic to Internet users, and which can win over investors and partners. These platforms create an 'alternative' image that promotes innovation and creativity, freed from the yoke of industrial logics and their implacable financial concerns, in favour of an elsewhere that is freely chosen and over which one has full control, and where financing is a matter of choice, of sharing ideas and of love at first sight. On KissKissBankBank, partnerships advertise themselves under the philosophy of 'Do It Yourself' and co-creation. The partners are instead called 'mentors', and only their logos are shown. Other platforms like Indiegogo promote the concept of 'DIWO' (Do It With Others)—a gesture at the ideology of collective intelligence mentioned earlier.

Finally, if platforms are considered to be, or even legitimated as, 'alternatives' to bank lending institutions that are reluctant to invest in innovative cultural projects, they nevertheless have close links with those very institutions. There has been some degree of overlap since their creation, because banking partners and online payment services like PayPal handle transactions, claiming a percentage on each one (which varies depending on platform and payment method). For instance, Ulule has a partnership with BNP Paribas: 'Convinced that crowdfunding and bank financing complement each other, Ulule offers to refer you to BNP Paribas for all complementary needs relating to your entrepreneurial project financed on Ulule.'[5] KissKissBankBank initially had a partnership with La Banque Postale, which went on to acquire the platform in 2017. Far from being 'alternatives', these apparatuses now present themselves as tools which complement existing sources of credit. Indeed, banks may agree to finance projects once they have attained the required threshold. Success in crowdfunding, supported by a community of 'backers', becomes a means of preliminary screening that reduces the risk of lending.

## Apparatuses for Political and Legislative Action

Private-public relations are strengthened by political involvement and the development of the legislative frameworks necessary for these platforms to expand and diversify their domains of activity. In the United States, Obama's 2012 Jobs Act provided for regulated financial exchanges through these platforms, but also allowed them to extend the domain of their activities, for example allowing them to offer equity or investment in companies (Cunningham 2012).

Since 2013, numerous European countries have also adopted legislation aimed both at regulating these funding methods and allowing their potential expansion to other economic sectors (Dushnitsky et al. 2016).

In France, the extension of these forms of financing to domains beyond culture only became possible with the political support of subsequent ministers for sustainable development, economy and finance, including Montebourg, Moscovici and Macron. Marine Joaun's thesis (2017) demonstrates just how effective lobbying can be, particularly in deciding which platforms are authorised.

The ruling published in the *Journal Officiel* of 31 May 2014, which regulates platforms and authorizes exemptions from financial monopoly regulations, has officially recognised two specialized types of platforms:

- Loan platforms which finance diverse (often 'community-based' or 'entrepreneurial') projects via free or paid-for credit, collectively agreed by contributors-lenders.
- Investment platforms which primarily specialize in funding 'entrepreneurial' projects by issuing equity or debt securities, and whose reward for contributors-subscribers is a share in the potential profits of the project.

Finally, the importance of political backing can also be seen in France's promotion of heritage and cultural production by introducing special measures for crowdfunded projects. The most important of these are tax reductions for individuals and companies if their project is non-profit (with charitable status) or heritage-related.

Although digital activities potentially offer these platforms international visibility, we should note that, in reality, they are subject to national laws and regulations. The first platforms, representatives of the devolved modalities of the web, aimed at an international scale—the web being, in the minds of its creators, a network without borders. And yet, beyond all the talk, this internationalist dimension still depends on international and bilateral agreements between the countries concerned, as well as individual states' fiscal policies (VAT, income tax, copyright, consumers' rights). And no matter the country, project creators are legally subject to tax. Although legislation is often vague and not always strictly applied, the sums obtained when funding is successful can be considered revenue. As shown in the recommendations of the report 'Crowdfunding Schemes in Europe' (Rothler and Wenzlaff 2011), approaches in Europe still depend on the legislation of each member state, and remain to be harmonized.

It is therefore easy to understand the efforts made by these platforms and a number of private and/or public initiatives to inform legislators and the public, and so create national and international synergies in order to internationalize and globalize the 'ecosystem'. This is the case, for example, with the research carried out in the framework of the European Union funded CrowdFunding4Culture (http://www.crowdfunding4culture.eu), piloted by the private consultancy Idea Consult. The aim of this was to propose the development and, above all, the harmonization of these platforms at a European level. Similar initiatives have also been set up in the countries of the 'South'. In Africa, for example, the South African based ACfA (African Crowdfunding Association), created in 2015, aims to unify the activities of the continent's platforms and to remove the legislative barriers preventing monetary exchanges in or among other African countries.

The relationship between crowdfunding and politics depends on the use made of it by parties, unions and certain politicians. Use of these platforms or apparatuses typically brings up debates around their place in the participative democracy movement. We will discuss two distinct examples. The first—often cited by the high priests of cyberspace and other apologists for digital progress as a reference case for the 'revolutions' made possible by digital technologies—is the use of such funding in Obama's first presidential campaign. In 2008, Obama appealed to the generosity of his supporters to partly fund his campaign, raising $150 million. But this was only a tiny part of the total, and exponential, cost of the campaign. In this first case, crowdfunding served more as a showcase and a communications operation, rather than having any significant impact on the 'democratic experience'. A second example, closer to home, took place in March 2018. On the initiative of the sociologist Jean-Marc Salmon, supported by twenty or so artists and intellectuals, an appeal for donations was launched on the 'money pot' site Leetchi to set up a strike fund to support the continuation of the movement against SNCF reforms. By 18 May 2018, 28,907 donors had given €1,132,001. This second example highlights all the ambiguities of the apparatus. Although it enabled financial support for political opposition, it also contributed indirectly to the development of the very same liberal economic logics that workers were fighting against.


## Platforms as Technical Apparatuses

As we have stated above, the element that characterizes this type of platform is the establishment of a technical apparatus, in the sense defined by the philosopher Giorgio Agamben (2009). Crowdfunding platforms are above all a matter of coding. They are carefully planned out before going live, giving users access to services and to a particular organization of information. Without revisiting the large quantity of debate and research on the relations between techniques and uses, one should recall that coding intervenes upstream of content and the participation of project creators and backers. Platforms for cultural finance determine the framework for their automated services, from registering on the site to participating as a project creator, a contributor of ideas and knowledge or a backer. In doing so, the platforms establish how they will function (Flichy 2008): they must be ergonomic, intuitive and easy to use. It can be very damaging, for instance, if it takes too many clicks to reach the required information or to make a payment, as this discourages backers from finalizing their donation. The platforms also aggregate and exploit user data (partly visible on the statistics pages the platforms provide) and develop dedicated APIs (Application Programming Interfaces) which allow the platform, for example, to run as white label products on other businesses' sites.

Algorithmic automation is also at work in content promotion on the site—for instance, which projects are featured will vary depending on the viewer's tastes and location. As apparatuses, these platforms make information and content visible while selecting material according to prior editorial decisions. By promoting certain projects on their homepage or personalizing what they show users depending on their actions on the site, they contribute to the hierarchization of information and reinforce competition between projects.

Like any apparatus, platforms legally establish and normalize administrative procedures (General Terms and Conditions of Use) and the relations between players who will subsequently interact according to a logic of 'co-innovation'. The sociologist Emile Gayoso (2015) remarks that: co-innovation platforms work on both sides at once (innovation, management and marketing) and in this sense give us a privileged vantage point on the re-embedding of business within society which, as managerial injunction but also as structural necessity, has taken shape in the Western world following the crisis of the 70s, with the growth of the 'networked business' and of 'management by project' (Boltanski and Chiapello 1999), and finds in the Internet a powerful catalyst.

## Platforms for Artists and Creation?

'Free your creativity', declares the participative platform KissKissBankBank. Kickstarter's homepage is emblazoned with the words 'Discover creative projects'. Patreon offers to help you 'regain your creative freedom', while the British platform PledgeMusic has described itself as 'a unique marketplace where fans and artists connect'. Given such slogans, it is no wonder the media, politicians, as well as many other social actors, appear to be infatuated with crowdfunding. These words, and the platforms which produce them, are symptomatic of current discourse on the digital economy, inviting 'creatives' to participate, to mobilize communities and to revitalize project funding and, more globally, culture itself.

The confusion between the terms 'creation', 'creativity' and 'projects' are symptomatic of the creative industries (Tremblay 2010; Hesmondhalgh 2008) and their attempts to create value by evacuating the aesthetic and artistic issues distinctive to artistic creation, instead emphasizing individual creativity as an end in itself. Crowdfunding platforms posit themselves as new cultural intermediaries, opening the way to new possibilities for 'supporting creation'. The issue here is the valorization of 'making' without the need for any kind of 'knowing', and the celebration of creativity to the detriment of any aesthetic or theoretical considerations.

In music, literature and cinema, the discourses circulated by project creators reinforce this positioning, both through the attention they pay to these logics and the way they represent them. We see an example of this with the following author, who submitted a book project to a French platform:

> At first I sent my manuscript to publishing houses, but with hindsight I can see that was never going to work. They looked at the style first of all, and it's true, it wasn't good enough. I tried again with a second manuscript, and this time I got more notes. But still they told me that it didn't fit into their current publication priorities. A friend told me about this platform, and I tried signing up. I don't know much about it, but I said to myself, why not. (T, 27 years old, book project)

Another user proposed an album:

> I saw it [financial participation] as a funding method which meant you could get a project going which just wouldn't happen by traditional routes. I saw it as a form of funding in advance. (T, 25 years old, music project)

Most of those we spoke to saw these platforms in this way, as potential means to finance and complete their projects, with various possible alterations depending on the pledges received.

> Honestly, I didn't think it was going to work. I didn't think people would be willing to give like that. I told myself I'd give it a try, and I reached my goal in a week! [The target was €2,000.] If I'd have known, I'd have asked for €10,000! [...] In actual fact, I got more than that. It'll be enough for me to make more projects, a bigger book, a larger print run. (F, 32 years old, book project)

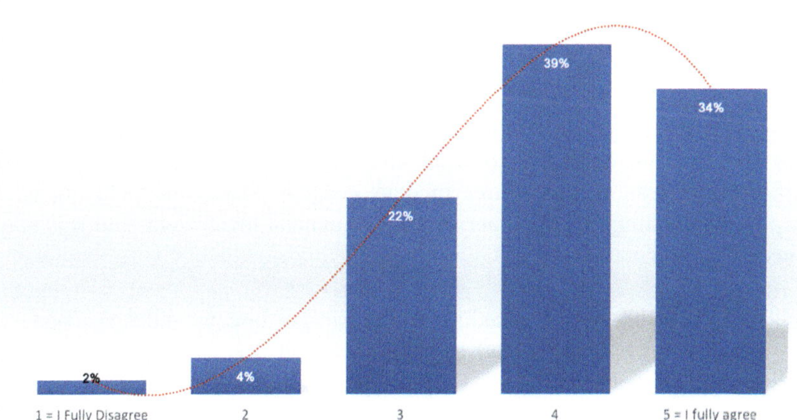


**Figure 3:** Source: ANR Collab 2017.

Our qualitative study (including both citizens who had participated in or financed a project, and those who had not) further supported the idea that crowdfunding platforms help ensure cultural diversity.

Projects on these platforms are not dependent on the restrictive, pyramidal selection logics of cultural industries. At first sight, they therefore seem less subject to economic or aesthetic demands, and free from the pressure of institutional sponsors and backers. Remember that most of those who pledge money to a project have a direct link of some sort to the project creator, either as family or friends, and usually do not monitor the production and development of the project carefully. This absence of control is counterbalanced by the 'exclusive' rewards which backers receive, and which are dependent on the amount they pledge. Our research shows that the projects proposed—and the desires of the creators themselves—typically do not aim at novelty or aesthetic experimentation, but rather the success of the campaign and the satisfaction of a personal pleasure, the symbolic achievement of 'having done it' (Flichy 2010). Note that the issues are somewhat different for project creators who are not entirely amateur. The alternative on offer is to fund a project without getting involved in commercial, professional and contractual logics—instead, one can take an alternative, DIY approach. This last point is essential, for this is how project creators can guarantee control of the object financed, as well as associated rights:

I wanted to make something good. Why bring it out as a CD? Personally, I never buy CDs, unless I buy them after a concert I enjoyed. That's the

> kind of spirit I started the project with, not in the spirit of a distributor
> like Harmonia Mundi or Naive who was going to distribute it … I did
> it for myself, to have something to distribute to people who come to see
> me and sometimes ask if they can buy a CD. (V, musical project creator,
> 35 years old)

As in the financing stages of traditional cultural or audio-visual projects, the alternative seems to be not so much an alternative approach to 'creation' or diffusion. Instead, it is as an intermediate phase in which one seeks financial support, including making a personal and financial investment, and this may succeed or fail.

> Well, it's good that we asked for too much. For one, we didn't manage
> to get as much as we wanted, but then there were people who contacted
> us afterwards because of it. People who came to it a bit late. So even
> though it failed, we tried, and now it also means that we're better known.
> (Musician, 45 years old)

Certain skills beyond the 'creative' talents specific to the project itself are needed for a successful crowdfunding campaign. Prescribed by the platforms (see chapter 3) and largely self-taught, these are basically marketing and communications skills. In terms of project management, they primarily involve creating and activating the network, generating a sense of, and creating and managing a community (Matthews, Rouzé and Vachet 2014; see digital appendixes, chapter 5). While crowdfunding is often presented as an alternative to the restrictive logics of the cultural industries, in this respect it seems more like a publicity and communications tool which drives other types of promotion.

This dimension of communications and publicity is well illustrated by museums. In turning to these modes of financing, museums aim to increase the visibility of their projects, and to build loyal communities around them. For instance, the Centre des Monuments Nationaux used the platform MyMajorCompany to collect funds for the restoration of a number of historical monuments, including Mont St. Michel. Ulule has hosted projects by the Musée d'Orsay and the Musée de la Marine. In the United States, the Smithsonian, MoMA, and the Marina Abramovic Institute have all used Kickstarter campaigns to restore or finance projects on various scales.

In France, as part of its policy for digital modernization baptized 'the digital Louvre', the Louvre has created an internal platform, 'Tous Mécènes', to publicize its restoration projects and to create a community of patrons to take on activities that were formerly the province of groups like the 'friends of the museum' (Mairesse 2016). Note that these campaigns should be understood more broadly, in the context of a network of injunctions that go beyond the question of funding innovations alone. In the heritage sector, for example, in 2007 Joëlle Le Marec conceptualized the modernist injunction to the museum to 'get moving' (Le Marec 2007, 169) and to be digitally up to date as a structural logic at work transversally across institutions, their services and their projects. Far from being an alternative, the use of such platforms is above all strategic. The opinions of members of staff may differ, and they might not always see such initiatives in a positive light.

## Conclusion

As a conclusion, we would like to return to the significance and role of these platforms in the development of culture. Although they allow some projects to meet their goals, or partial funding for more ambitious ones, many other projects are held back by the forms of competition involved and do not have such opportunities. This clearly calls into question their capacity to foster cultural diversity. The projects that will flourish are those that already boast a large community with sufficient financial resources, whose tastes and cultural and social practices depend on their class allegiances (the impact of cultural capital, Bourdieu 1979) as well as their age range (generational impact) and their geographical location (Hugues and Peterson 1983). Our research shows that, apart from the class logic in play, and the inequalities in the distribution of backers and project creators across the country (see the conclusion to the preceding chapter), 'innovative technological projects' generate more interest and attract funding decisions, to the detriment of other cultural categories.

The same logic also favours projects which comply with pre-existing tastes and fashions, to the detriment of projects whose aesthetics, format, or concerns are remote from common preoccupations, or on the fringes of traditional or mainstream cultural expressions. This question is rendered still more acute by the ambiguity of the partnerships between private and public players, who support projects in line with their communications and marketing strategies and their own economic logics. Far from being alternatives to the logics and strategies of the cultural and creative industries, these platforms follow the logic of the capitalist ecosystem: stimulating competition between projects, and contributing to competitive hierarchizations of projects which are correlated with the necessity of rendering them visible, a process reinforced by inegalitarian forms of access and sharing (size of community, social origins, etc.). Finally, as we saw above in the case of the 2018 appeal to fund the rail workers' strike in France, it raises questions around the systematic integration of any alternative or protest movement, a mechanism necessary to the survival of the capitalist economy (Boltanski and Chiapello 2018).

Far from being alternatives, today's platforms are newly integrated links in the cultural sector. By way of the ecosystems they work to create and/or strengthen, they produce complementarities between different players in various economic and institutional sectors, and also seek to federate others. A competitive logic nevertheless endures in this 'collaborative' market, contributing to the growth of rivalry between platforms but also, and above all, between projects and between project creators—far from a logic of equitable participation or of the commons. They therefore contribute to what Lash and Lury (2007) have called the culturization of the economy, by placing the 'experience' of the consumer/citizen (defending a project, raising funds for it, participating in its success) as well as the 'local' dimension (a strategic element of what some economists call the 'purple' economy) at the heart of a system supposedly dependent on innovation and brand-based capitalization.

## Notes

[1] https://tousnosprojets.bpifrance.fr/Observatoire/(type)/don Accessed April 1st 2019.

[2] *Ambition numérique: pour une politique française et européenne de la transition numérique [Digital Ambition: for a French and European Policy of Digital Transition]*, report of the Conseil National du Numérique, 2015.

[3] One should stress however that these different models and strategies are not fully exclusive, as some platforms borrow from one or another model.

[4] In France, the *fonds de dotation* is one such endowment, dedicated to works or missions of 'general interest' or to assisting other non-profit organizations to accomplish such missions. The base amount needed to set up a *fonds de dotation* has been set at €15,000 by law.

[5] https://nl.ulule.com/bnpparibas/#/ Accessed November 18th 2018.

## References


Agamben, Giorgio. 2009. *What is an Apparatus?*, trans. by David Kishik and Stefan Pedatella. Redwood City, CA: Stanford University Press.

Anderson, Chris. 2006. *The Long Tail: Why the Future of Business is Selling More for Less*. New York: Hyperion.

Banks, Mark, Rosalind Gill and Stephanie Taylor. 2013. *Theorizing Cultural Work: Labour, Continuity and Change in the Cultural and Creative Industries*. London: Routledge.

Barthes, Roland. 1972. *Mythologies*, trans. by Annette Lavers. New York: Farrar, Straus & Giroux.

Bauwens, Michel, & Kostakis, Vasilis. (2014). From the Communism of Capital to Capital for the Commons: Towards an Open Co-operativism. *tripleC: Communication, Capitalism & Critique*, 12(1), 356–61.

Boltanski, Luc, and Eve Chiapello. 2018. *The New Spirit of Capitalism*, 2nd edn., trans. by Gregory Elliott. London: Verso.

Bouquillion, Phillipe, and Jacob T. Matthews. 2010. *Le Web collaboratif: mutations des industries de la culture et de la communication.* Grenoble: Presses Universitaires de Grenoble.

Bourdieu, Pierre. 1979. *Distinction: A Social Critique of the Judgment of Taste,* trans. by Richard Nice. Cambridge, MA: Harvard University Press.

Bourreau, Marc and Michel Gensollen. 2006. L'Impact d'Internet et des Technologies de l'Information et de la Communication sur l'Industrie de la Musique Enregistrée. *Revue d'Économie Industrielle,* 116: 31–70.

Bullich. Vincent. 2015. Régulation des pratiques amateurs et accompagnement de la professionnalisation: la stratégie de YouTube dans la course aux contenus exclusifs, *Les Enjeux de l'Information et de la Communication,* 6.3b, 27–42, <https://lesenjeux.univ-grenoble-alpes.fr/2015-supplementB/02-Bullich/index.html> [accessed 27 February 2019].

Cardon, Dominique. 2010. *La Démocratie internet: promesses et limites.* Paris: Seuil.

Cassella, Milena, and Francesco D'Amato. 2014. Crowdfunding Music: The Value of Social Networks and Social Capital in Participatory Music Production, in *Civilizations 13: The State of the Music Industry/L'État de l'industrie musicale,* ed. by in Victor Sarafian and Rosie Findley. Toulouse: Presses de l'Université Toulouse 1 Capitole, pp. 93–122.

Conseil National du Numérique. 2015. Ambition numérique: pour une politique française et européenne de la transition numérique.

Corcuff, Philippe. 1998. Justification, Stratégie et Compassion: Apport de la Sociologie des Régimes d'Action. *Correspondance. Bulletin d'information scientifique de l'Institut de recherche sur le Maghreb contemporain.* Available at http://boltanski.chez-alice.fr/texte/corcuff.pdf [last accessed 26 June 2019]

Cunningham, William Michael. 2012. The Jobs Act, in *The Jobs Act: Crowdfunding for Small Businesses and Startups.* Berkeley, CA: Apress, pp. 3 20.

Direction de l'Animation de la Recherche, des Études et des Statistiques (DARES). 2017. *L'économie des plateformes: Enjeux pour la croissance, le travail, l'emploi et les politiques publiques.* Available at https://dares.travail-emploi.gouv.fr/IMG/pdf/de_2013_economie_collaborative.pdf  [lastr accessed 5 March 2019]

Doan, AnHai, Raghu Ramakrishnan and A.Y. Halevy. 2011. Crowdsourcing Systems on the World-Wide Web, *Communications of the ACM,* 54(4), 86–96.

Downing John H. 2001. *Radical Media: Rebellious Communication and Social Movements.* London: Sage.

Dushnitsky, Gary, Massimiliana Guerini, Evila Piva, and Cristina Rossi-Lamastra. 2016. Crowdfunding in Europe: Determinants of Platform Creation Across Countries, *California Management Review,* 58(2), 44–71.

Eisenmann, Thomas, Geoffrey Parker and Marshall W. Van Alstyne. 2006. Strategies for Two-Sided Markets, *Harvard Business Review,* 84(10), 92.

Farchy, Joëlle, and Dominique Sagot-Duvauroux. 1994. *Économie des politiques culturelles*. Paris: PUF.

Flichy, Patrice. 2008. Technique, usage et représentations, *Réseaux* 2–3 (148–9), 147–174.

———. 2010. *Le Sacre de l'amateur: sociologie des passions ordinaires à l'ère numérique*. Paris: Seuil.

Friedman, Thomas. 2005. *The World is Flat: A Brief History of the Globalized World in the 21st Century*. London: Allen Lane.

Fuchs, Christian. 2010. Alternative Media as Critical Media. *European Journal of Social Theory*, 13(2), 173–92

———. 2014. *Digital Labour and Karl Marx*. London: Routledge.

———. 2017. Reflections on Michael Hardt and Antonio Negri's Book 'Assembly', *tripleC: Communication, Capitalism & Critique*, 15(2): 851–65

Garnham, Nicholas. 2005. From Cultural to Creative Industries: An Analysis of the Implications of the 'Creative Industries' Approach to Arts and Media Policy Making in the United Kingdom, *International Journal of Cultural Policy*, 11(1), 15–29.

Gayoso, Émile. 2015. Les plateformes de co-innovation, *Réseaux*, 2, 121–149.

Gillespie, Tarleton. 2010. The Politics of Platforms, *New Media & Society*, 12(3), 347–364.

Greco, Thomas. 2001. *Money: Understanding and Creating Alternatives to Legal Tender*. White River Junction: Chelsea Green Publishing.

Grosman, Anna and Ana Brandes 2015. Crowdfunding and Innovation: IBM in Berg Grell, K., Marom, D. and Swart, R. *Crowdfunding: The Corporate Era*. London: Elliott & Thompson, pp. 124–136.

Hardt, Michael, and Antonio Negri. 2001. *Empire*. Cambridge, MA: Harvard University Press.

———. 2017. *Assembly*. Oxford: Oxford University Press.

Hebdige, Dick. 1979. *Subculture: The Meaning of Style*. London: Routledge.

Hesmondhalgh, David. 2008. Cultural and Creative Industries, in Tony Bennett and John Frow (eds.), *The SAGE Handbook of Cultural Analysis*. London: Sage.

Hughes, Michael, and Richard A. Peterson. 1983. Isolating Cultural Choice Patterns in the US Population, *American Behavioral Scientist*, 26(4), 459–78.

Jouan, Marine. 2017. *La Construction sociale du marché du crowdfunding en France*. Doctoral dissertation, Telecom ParisTech.

Kruse, Holly. 1993. Subcultural Identity in Alternative Music Culture. *Popular Music*, 12(1): 33–41.

Langley, Paul. 2016. Crowdfunding in the United Kingdom: A Cultural Economy. *Economic Geography*, 92(3): 301–21.

Lash, Scott, and Celia Lury. 2007. *Global Culture Industry: The Mediation of Things*. Cambridge: Polity.

Latouche, Serge. 2014. *Sortir de la Société de Consommation: Voix et Voies de la Décroissance*. Paris: Éditions Les Liens Qui Libèrent.

Leguern Philippe (ed.). 2016. *Où va la Musique ? Numérimorphose et Nouvelles Expériences d'Écoute*, Paris: Presse des Mines.

Le Marec, Joëlle. 2007. *Publics et musées: la confiance éprouvée*. Paris: l'Harmattan.

Lebraty, Jean-Fabrice, and Katia Lobre-Lebraty. 2015. *Crowdsourcing: porté par le foule*. London: ISTE Editions.

Le Marec, Joëlle. 2007. *Publics et musées: la confiance éprouvée*. Paris: l'Harmattan.

Löwy, M. 2005. What is Ecosocialism?. *Capitalism Nature Socialism*, 16(2): 15–24.

Mairesse, François. 2016. Les modèles participatifs dans les musées, in *Crowdfunding, industries culturelles et démarche participative*, ed. by Laurent Creton and Kira Kitsopanidou. Bern: Peter Lang, pp. 99–113.

Matthews, Jacob. (2015a). Passé, présent et potentiel des plateformes collaboratives Réflexions sur la production culturelle et les dispositifs d'intermédiation numérique in *Les Enjeux de l'Information et de la Communication*. (16)1:57–71.

Matthews, Jacob. (2015b). Like a Fraction of Some Bigger Place: The 'Creative Industries' in a Peripheral Zone. Reflections from a Case Study', in *tripleC: Communication, Capitalism and Critique* (13)1. DOI:10.31269/triplec.v13i1.663

Matthews, Jacob, Vincent Rouzé and Jérémy Vachet. 2014. *La Culture par les foules? Le Crowdfunding en question*. Paris: MKF Editions.

Miège, Bernard. 2017. *Les Industries culturelles et créatives face à l'ordre de l'information et de la communication*. Grenoble: Presses de l'Université de Grenoble.

NESTA. 2013. *The Rise of Future Finance: The UK Alternative Finance Benchmarking Report*. London: NESTA.

———. 2014. *Understanding Alternative Finance: The UK Alternative Finance Industry Report 2014*. London: NESTA.

Newman, Michael Z. 2009. Indie Culture: In Pursuit of the Authentic Autonomous Alternative. *Cinema Journal*, 16–34.

Rochet, Jean-Charles, and Jean Tirole. 2006. Two-Sided Market: A Progress Report, *The RAND Journal of Economics*, 35(3), 645–667.

Rothler, David, and Karsten Wenzlaff. 2011. *Crowdfunding Schemes in Europe*. EENC Report, vol. 9.

Rouzé, Vincent, and Jacob Matthew. 2018. Les plateformes de crowdfunding culturel: entre figures de l'artiste entrepreneur et entrepreneurs polymorphes, *Les Enjeux de l'information et de la communication*, <https://lesenjeux.univ-grenoble-alpes.fr/2018/03-Rouze-Matthews/> [accessed 27 February 2019].

Sandoval, Marisol and Christian Fuchs. 2010.Towards a Critical Theory of Alternative Media. *Telematics and Informatics*, 27: 141–50.

Scholz, Trebor (ed.). 2012. *Digital Labor: The Internet as Playground and Factory*. London and New York: Routledge.

Scholz, Trebor. 2016. *Platform Cooperativism: Challenging the Corporate Sharing Economy*. New York: Rosa Luxemburg Foundation.

Stemler, Abbey R. 2013. The JOBS Act and Crowdfunding: Harnessing the Power—and Money—of the Masses, *Business Horizons*, 56(3), 271–275

Tapscott, Don, and Anthony D. Williams. 2008. *Wikinomics: How Mass Collaboration Changes Everything*. London: Penguin.

Thuillas, Oliver, and Louis Wiart. 2019. Plateformes Alternatives et Coopération d'Acteurs: Quels Modèles d'Accès aux Contenus Culturels?' *tic&société*, 13(1–2: 13–41. Available at http://journals.openedition.org/ticetsociete/3043. DOI: https://doi.org/10.4000/ticetsociete.3043 [ last accessed 26 June 2019].

Tremblay, Gaëtan. 2008. Industries culturelles, économie créative et société de l'information, *Global Media Journal*: Canadian Edition. (1)1: 65–88.

CHAPTER 4

# Participatory Cultural Platforms and Labour

Jacob Matthews and Vincent Rouzé

Our relationship to work, culture and knowledge seems to have been significantly altered by the rise of digital communications technologies. The neologism 'Uberization', derived from the web platform Uber, has become an apt term for the movement toward a so-called 'collaborative' economy in which salaried jobs no longer exist. At the same time, many of today's platforms encourage the valuing of individual 'creativity', something that reshapes the definition of the artist and creative work.

In this chapter we examine the impact of these platforms on our relationship to labour, its reorganization and the shift toward a project-based model of work (Jaillet-Roman 2002). It seems to us that these platforms and the apparatuses they deploy raise broader issues about 'creativity' and the collaborative economy, as well as the type of labour involved both inside and on the platforms. As Fuchs (2014), Scholz (2012), Cardon and Cassilli (2015), and Simonet (2015) have shown, the activities conducted on digital platforms belong to the category of *digital labour*, and as such are subject to new forms of labour organization and exploitation (Dujarier 2014), including forms of 'free' labour (Terranova 2000) that may constitute a 'cybertariat' (Huws 2003 and 2014). In addressing the platforms from this perspective, we hope to enrich the existing literature,

---

**How to cite this book chapter:**
Matthews, J. and Rouzé, V. 2019. Participatory Cultural Platforms and Labour. In: Rouzé, V. (ed.) *Cultural Crowdfunding: Platform Capitalism, Labour and Globalization.* Pp. 59–78. London: University of Westminster Press. DOI: https://doi.org/10.16997/book38.d. License: CC-BY-NC-ND 4.0

which largely focuses on the supposedly unprecedented ways these platforms operate (Divard 2013; Boyer et al. 2016), on their capacity to act as tools for 'liberation' and 'value sharing' (Lemoine 2014) in the name of technological and socio-economic innovation (Kuppuswamy and Bayus 2013) and cultural diversity (Fohr 2016), and on participants' motivations and the benefits they receive (Brabham 2009; Céré, Roth and Petavy 2015). We take a critical stance, examining platforms, players and their accompanying discourses in terms that go beyond gauging their functional effectiveness. To do so, we adopt a 'dynamic holistic' stance which pays attention to the way in which individual and collective behaviours are determined by structures and institutions, but also to social actors' proactive capacities (Vercellone 2008: 7). From a structural point of view, it's important to recognise that the platform economy relies not principally on commercial revenue deriving from the production of goods and services, but on a model stemming from the fields of advertising and finance; 'commissions' are justified by their ability to link up individuals and/or groups with commercial entities, brands or investment opportunities. And from an etymological point of view, the platform is indeed a space dedicated to the stationing of carriages that are to be unloaded or loaded with goods or persons: the platform constitutes a locus of transaction and translation – an instrument of ideological convergence.

In enthusiastic accounts, the platform economy is based on a worldwide market, open to a multitude of player of all sizes, linked together by digital networks. The regular emergence of new markets and conversion of users into economic players gives this project an allure of realisation – as long as one ignores the fact that a powerful oligopoly has emerged (Smyrnaios, 2017), and that even fringe players objectively dominate individual users. Moreover, we have shown that web platforms innovate mainly by reducing costs and allowing for an 'alteration of perceptions' that the various players have of the capitalisation process and the internal organisation of economic sectors (Matthews and Vachet, 2014).

Kenney and Zysman (2016) identify as privately generated platform-based 'ecosystems', companies which fundamentally 'are not delivering technology to their customers and clients—they use technology to deliver labour to them' (Smith and Leberstein 2015, 3). Moreover, it is apparent that the 'bargaining power of workers is undermined by the size and scope of the global market for labour; the anonymity that the digital medium affords is a double-edged sword, facilitating some types of economic inclusion, but also allowing employers to discriminate at will' (Graham, Hjorth and Lehdonvirta 2017: 16). And as De Stefano points out 'the possibility of being easily terminated via a simple deactivation or exclusion from a platform or app may magnify the fear of retaliation that can be associated to non-standard forms of work, in particular temporary ones' (De Stefano 2016: 10).

These perspectives in turn us to consider the phenomenon of crowdfunding in the light of the constraints and opportunities it presents for the productive activities of the artist as 'project creator'—a version of the 'artist as labourer' figure proposed by Menger (2002)—as well as the characteristic of the other players involved, and in particular the work of those who manage platforms. Our hypothesis is that both emerge as 'polymorphous entrepreneurs'. At the intersection of multiple, often contradictory players and logics, their work consists fundamentally in trying to synthesize them so as to optimize the economic value extraction upon which their livelihood depends. This hypothesis converges with that of Marine Jouan who, following the works of Bergeron, Castel and Nouguez (2013), introduces the notion of a 'border-entrepreneur', defined by their position 'on the border of many worlds in tension', and their strategic reshaping of these into a 'new world of which they will be the centre' (Jouan 2017: 335).

This chapter is divided into three complementary parts. In the first we analyze the structural modifications of labour carried out by and on these platforms, and the representations they produce. In the second, we focus specifically on the forms of labour organization deployed within platforms, and examine how the work of project creators and members of their 'community' is framed and optimized, before considering how this process echoes platform managers' efforts to optimize their own projects and communities. Finally, the third part develops the hypothesis that platforms (and their various uses) can be understood as instruments of ideological production; to do this we analyze the 'pedagogical mission' emphasized in the guidelines issued by many platforms.

## Towards Gamification, or Invisible Labour

Human activities that take place on and around these platforms are obviously embedded in commercial relationships, and cannot escape the transformation of labour power into commodities, one of the fundamental characteristics of capitalism. And yet, in the case of cultural production financed through crowdfunding platforms, this transformation does not take place by way of a salaried workforce (which indeed has long been the case in the media and culture industries, where salaried jobs are the exception rather than the rule). Consequently, these apparatuses apparently consolidate pre-existing forms of labour organization, in particular by extending them to encompass cultural workers who had previously been spared to some extent, either because they were somewhat protected by public institutions or because their 'amateur' practices still put up some resistance to commodification and industrialization. It should also be recognized that intermediation apparatuses existed within the cultural field long before the emergence of crowdfunding and crowdsourcing platforms.

Nevertheless, what is most characteristic of cultural crowdfunding is its capacity to extend commercial prospecting into specific areas of cultural production, including alternative, or even oppositional, creative labour, and places where production merges into 'social' or 'community economies', drawing these different forms into an eminently 'entrepreneurial' project-based model through the consecration of the figure of the artist as 'project creator'. Secondly, if platforms do indeed bring about a structural modification of labour, they now do so, as Marine Jouan's (2017) research suggests, in an entirely ideological way, acting as 'pathfinders': that is, although they no longer fundamentally transform labour *per se*, they show the way.

The hypothesis can be sharpened by looking into the terms used to define and circumscribe the phenomenon. The idea of 'crowdfunding', like 'crowdsourcing', refers to the idea of a corporate sponsor outsourcing tasks to the 'crowd' (Lebraty and Lobre-Lebraty 2015). Note once more that the current resurgence of the word 'crowd' not only implies the erasure of the singularity of each supposed member, but also tends to remove all trace of structural economic, social and cultural inequalities between those who purportedly make up this crowd. As suggested in preceding chapters, platforms are constructed as intermediation apparatuses and therefore as apparatuses for the mobilization of disparate players thus committed to 'collaborating' together. In this sense, they also set themselves up as the real drivers of the logics of trans-media convergence somewhat enthusiastically highlighted by Henry Jenkins (2006).

This mobilization is promoted by a profusion of evangelical technophile discourses consubstantial with the 'collaborative web' (Bouquillon and Matthews 2010), which advocate ubiquity of access, the omnipotence of the network, sharing, and diversity of content for all—so long as it is strictly contained within the framework of assent for these means of communication and content as private property. These discourses would have us believe that, thanks to digital intermediation, everyone is now in a position to engage in new creative 'experiences'—experiences that blur the lines between production and consumption, as anticipated in the neologism 'prosumers', coined by the American futurologist Alvin Toffler in the 1980s. Alongside the promotion of personalized, individualized 'experience', all reference to labour as a social relation is gradually abandoned, even though it is this labour that enables the productive process and the capital accumulation realized through it. In this way, crowdsourcing and crowdfunding become original, indispensable methods for the creation, publicization and funding of cultural projects—methods that nevertheless remain entirely in line with the industrial strategies into which they are more or less obviously integrated. As entrepreneur and social media analyst Romain Péchan wrote in 2010 on OWNI's website, 'What is at stake for artists is no longer to produce, it is to face their audience, and to make sure this audience knows and recognizes them.'[1] What we see taking shape here is a metadiscourse produced by platforms as they attempt to mobilize labour (in 'creative' and other forms) without naming it, while dissimulating the inequalities and exploitation concomitant with it. The (free) participation of each person is foregrounded and capital is 'democratized', while all reference to labour as social relation, object of commercial exchange and site of conflict disappears entirely.

This form of ideology appears in the arguments of the researcher Sophie Renault (2014), who speaks of 'ludification' (or 'gamification') as a process of 'managerial innovation' characteristic of collaborative platforms. According to Renault, this notion—which in fact leads to a form of social engineering—designates the 'transfer of the mechanisms of the game into domains where they are not traditionally present'. She adds: 'The objective of gamification, which depends on the crowd's need for recognition, reward and amusement, is to influence the crowd's behaviour' (Renault 2014: 198). Here we find the elements of a fetishization of social reality that also helps call into question some fundamental oppositions and delimitations that appeared during early industrialization: the opposition between amateur and professional, and that between production and consumption. It is precisely within this optic that Patrice Flichy (2017) approaches digital labour in his book *Les Nouvelles Frontières du travail à l'ère du numérique* (The New Frontiers of Labour in the Digital Era) (2017). Although he gives a precise and lengthy description of the sociological constitution of this phenomenon based on a differentiation between work and leisure—all the better to establish how the lines between the two spheres have become blurred—he leaves aside the fact that this blurring of lines lies at the very heart of contemporary industrial strategies (particularly in the field of culture and communications). He can thus analyze the development of these platforms *ex nihilo*, as a vector of individual aspirations which promises greater entrepreneurial freedom to individuals. His analysis thus ends up very closely following the discourses and strategies developed by crowdfunding platforms, the promoters of digital *fintech* and, in general, the players of the 'collaborative' economy.

## Organizing and Optimizing Labour

Our analysis, on the contrary, sees digital intermediation apparatuses as instruments that enable a reconfiguration of the organization of labour, not in the sense of an emancipation of individuals, but, on the contrary, in the service of tried and tested capitalist logics. Under the cover of liberty and diversity, their primary aim is to optimize the various strata of a segmented production process, implicating all of the players involved.

### *1. Inside Platforms*

The first level of the organization of labour is carried out 'internally' by the platforms' managers. Its aim is to coordinate and optimize the work of their various direct 'collaborators': technical and logistical maintenance, research and development, the rollout and implementation of new services, finance and accounting, internal and external communications, particularly for the benefit of different users and partners, and so on. We should emphasize that, as in the creative industries (Banks et al. 2013; Hesmondalgh and Baker 2011), the workforce here is insecure, often made up of interns and freelance workers. This insecurity can extend even to directors, who are sometimes unable to award themselves a regular fixed salary. Our interviews with managers of crowdfunding platforms during the two research programmes mentioned in the introduction confirm how uncertain and anxiety-inducing such work can be, particularly for those with the least security. In parallel, this organization depends upon the automation of processes for registering and creating pages 'in a few clicks', promotion of content on the site (projects highlighted depending on the user's preferences or location, for example), automated aggregation and exploitation of user data (partly visible on the statistics pages the platforms provide), and the development of dedicated APIs (Application Programming Interfaces). On this point, sociologist Émile Gayoso emphasizes that platforms are technical objects made up of 'various programs brought together under a single interface'; 'internally', they are used 'to manage the company's publications and the contributions of Internet users (content management), as well as communication between users (community management)' (Gayoso 2015: 127). It is at these second and third levels that a *de facto* 'external' organization of labour is carried out *by* and *on* the platform.

### *2. Project Creators*

The second level consists in the work of controlling and regulating the material that project creators bring to the platform. Firstly, according to an editorial logic that may be more or less strict, this material is screened (even before being accepted on the platform) and its 'feasibility' is gauged—something that takes into account the project's 'maturity', the size of the existing community, the proposed duration of the campaign, the amount requested, and so on. As an example, the 'refused projects' section of KissKissBankBank says: 'We refuse personal projects (vacations, honeymoons, birthdays, funding of a loan…). For projects that meet the criteria of creativity, innovation, or community value, the credibility and seriousness of the project must be clearly expressed in order for it to be presented on the site.'

On the pretext of ensuring the success of a project, the platforms then assist in the normalization of work processes. From this point on, the user's activities now function in an undifferentiated, and rarely individualized, way. In our interviews, 70% of project creators said that the platform they submitted their project to did not help them during the campaign. Where help is given, it is via 'recommendations' and suggestions available online. Ulule offers project creators 'five golden rules for a successful project'. KissKissBankBank lists a series of rules for successful fundraising called 'the fundamentals', and presents a 'method' that strongly encourages project creators to conform to the production of normalized content: straplines, videos, or sequences of 'power-ful' images, 'effective' rewards, a 'credible' biography. According to the online guidance given by all platforms, success depends on at least three elements: networking, community building and the visibility of the project. Figures are also presented to rationalize the progress of a successful campaign: if a project reaches 30% of the total requested within the first week, it has more chance of success than otherwise. It seems to us that many of these FAQs suggest what an 'ideal' crowdfunding campaign looks like, and encourage users to follow this pattern. A set of normalized organizational processes emerge, often in the form of questions. Project creators are nonetheless free to ignore them. This is how we can read the following declaration by Jean-Sébastien Noël, co-founder of the Quebec platform La Ruche: 'You're not obliged to do it, but I'd strongly recommend it to anyone'. Our quantitative study confirms this proposition is a prerequisite for a campaign's success. If we compare the variables representing a campaign's success with the variable representing whether or not it followed the platform's guidelines, it seems that the chances of success or failure are mixed. However, in the case of video production, it does seem that the rate of success is dependent on following the guideline.

What is characteristic of these 'recommendations' is that they blur the lines between command and suggestion. The tasks to be accomplished are car-ried out in a devolved, outsourced way that may at first sight seem free of any injunction from above. But by making these 'recommendations' to project creators, platforms drive a normalization of 'how things are done' and what strategies should be adopted, and so develop a form of control over the whole experience, in the sense in which Deleuze (1995) understands the term 'con-trol'. Our qualitative and quantitative studies confirm that, depending on the project's profile, the amount of labour spent on it varies greatly (from less than five hours per week to over twenty). But we can show a net correlation between the number of hours spent on a campaign and its likelihood of success: a 21% success rate against a 2% failure rate when more than twenty hours per week are spent on the project. In all other cases, the failure rate is greater than the success rate.

What emerges is an obligation to dedicate at least twenty hours of labour per week to developing and promoting one's crowdfunding campaign, includ-ing during its preparation, when specific tasks must be carried out, including in particular the design and distribution of 'rewards'. As we can see from the responses of project creators, this work calls for multiple skills, including com-munication and marketing (cited by 63% of respondents), project management (55%), IT and/or graphic design (48%), and video editing (31%). These skills are often quite different from those the artistic project itself is based on, and are generally self-taught and/or supplied by appeals for help to members of the 'community'. Most project leaders we interviewed confirmed that such work causes significant stress (which, incidentally, undermines the supposedly 'ludic' nature of the process). Furthermore, none of this is any guarantee of success. In our study, 57% of project creators said that their campaign had been a failure, as opposed to 43% who reported success. The failures were most often attributed either to having requested too high an amount, or to problems reaching people beyond their immediate or extended family (family and friends of friends). In our interviews, respondents often 'owned up' to their responsibility for the campaign's failure, recognizing mistakes made in the development or implementation of their marketing strategy, and regretted not having better followed and/or understood the advice provided in the guidelines.

More generally, with the help of these tools and recommendations, platforms are achieving ever-higher rates of success. KissKissBankBank went from a 34% success rate in 58 projects launched in 2010, to a 70% success rate out of a total of 4,470 projects in 2017. Ulule has an overall success rate of 65%, while Kickstarter has a lower rate of 35.8%. Although success rates vary widely across different cultural sectors—depending on the mobilization of the available donors and the average amounts pledged—they testify above all to the success of simplified recommendations, and to the fact that platforms have an interest in emphasizing these recommendations yet further so as to optimize the number of successful campaigns and the fees earned from them.

### 3. The 'Community'

Lastly, on a third and more indirect 'external' level, we find the work of 'community management', which is largely outsourced to project creators. For a crowdfunding campaign to succeed, 'leverage' on digital social networks obviously has to be optimized. This remains one of the priorities of the various people who work for the platform. It is to be achieved by ensuring the ergonomics and fluidity of the site and its interconnection with external networks and players. Project creators have a clear role to play here, since it is up to them to launch the project, to maintain and increase the flow of donors and to ensure the everyday management of these 'communities'. They must make every effort to publicize their project; they are 'invited' to send regular updates through e-mail and social networks (Facebook, Twitter, Instagram, etc.) to family, friends and acquaintances, following a centripetal logic known as 'the three circles' (family and friends, acquaintances and the wider public). To attain the required 'levels', they must continually activate their network. But as in the model of the 'two step flow of communication' developed by Katz and Lazarsfeld (2017[1955]), it must be enriched by similar, redundant activities on the part of members of the 'community' who support the project. This labour is fundamental, since projects are hierarchized as a function of community activity, becoming more or less prominent on the site depending on quantitative variables defined by the management (support, fans, subscribers, likes, comments, etc.). Some players even define this regular, time-consuming involvement as a kind of 'art', which suggests that they must draw some benefit from elevating routine administrative processes into art forms, and raises significant questions about the real level of permeability between these two domains.

### 4. The Professional 'Ecosystem'

This mobilization of the community and these forms of networking are also pursued by the managers of platforms themselves, as they promote an image of (hyper)active 'start-uppers' constantly in search of new modes of financing and value creation. To this end, they actually make use of 'their' own platforms with the aim of developing extended and versatile social and professional networks. Marine Jouan describes this intense labour of networking:

> As it appeared on the media agenda, more and more players outside the world of crowdfunding asked themselves whether or not they should be using this funding method. [...] The objective of crowdfunding professionals is to get these players to forge partnerships with their platforms, so that players interested in crowdfunding do not start up their own platforms, increasing competition for the capture of projects and funds. (Jouan 2017: 337)

Jouan's research also insists on the importance of consolidating and extending existing networks, particularly by producing and disseminating supposed 'crowdfunding studies' and 'barometers'. In their 'desire to communicate', these discursive elements 'are conceived above all to create 'buzz' in the media, but also around events organized by the association [Crowdfunding France]' (Jouan 2017: 343). She lists two forms of partnership such activities aim at, both of which are undeniably reminiscent of professional community management. In the first case, the partner 'will direct toward the partner platform certain project leaders who are in its network and who are seeking funding', while 'the second type of partnership involves the transfer of the partner's funds to the campaigns on the platform' (Jouan 2017: 355). It is useful to compare these two ways of optimizing social networks, one of which is deployed by project creators, the other by platform managers, but both of which depend on constantly increasing and renewing traffic in order to avoid failure and maintain the momentum of their respective projects.

## Train, Educate, Agitate

We have emphasized that one of the characteristics of cultural crowdfunding is that, if it does not entirely overthrow all the classical codes and references of the 'worlds of art', it certainly erodes them—or, as we have written elsewhere, it gives a 'common language' to the different players connected by the platforms and, in doing so, contributes to shaping them as predominantly economic players (Matthews, Rouzé and Vachet 2014: 30). Most platform directors and managers insist on the 'pedagogical' work they have to do for project creators and certain 'communities' of backers. The objective here is to counteract the 'old' mentalities of cultural workers who are too dependent on systems of public grants (or 'assistance'), wary of going beyond their target audience, lacking in communication skills and unable to 'sell themselves'. We have observed how, beyond setting up the technical means to enhance the initiatives of project creators, platforms employ a discourse of the rationalization and commodification of the cultural sphere, and do their best to transform cultural workers into entrepreneurs. This discourse is disseminated on websites and social networks—but also through online and print publications, heavy coverage in traditional media, organizing and participating in public conferences, university education, and initiatives where certain project creators are recognized and given appearances at public events. Barely concealed in the invitation to 'become a part of an artistic, creative and innovative family' is a condemnation of those losers who don't know how to take advantage of these (necessarily 'neutral') new technologies.

### *1. Promotional Discourses*

Promoted by numerous players in business, the media, academia, and politics, it is supposedly certain that the crowdfunding model will spread and become a significant component in numerous economic sectors—a determination reflected in the extent of coverage in both print and online media (Benistant and Marty 2016). These discourses are echoed by the publication, in many countries, of dozens of didactic and popular works with evocative titles such as *A Crowdfunder's Strategy Guide: Build a Better Business by Building Community* (Stegmaier 2015), *Crowdfunding Basics in 30 Minutes: How to Use Kickstarter, Indiegogo, and Other Crowdfunding Platforms to Support Your Entrepreneurial and Creative Dreams* (Epstein 2018); *Le Crowdfunding: les rouages du crowdfunding* (Crowdfunding: The Mechanics of Crowdfunding) (Iizuka 2015); *Le Crowdfunding: mode d'emploi* (Crowdfunding: An Instruction Manual) (Hendrickx 2015), and *Crowdfunding: mener son projet* (Crowdfunding: Running Your Project) (Baudoire 2016). If we are to believe these various infatuated commentators, crowdfunding has become a 'must' for the funding of cultural production at an individual, community, industrial, and institutional level.

This enthusiastic discourse can take as evidence the continually improving economic performance of the platforms. In Europe, across 150 platforms including all forms of financing, the amounts raised grew to almost €3 billion in 2014—a growth of 146% on 2012.[2] According to the BPI, 80% of the money raised came from UK platforms. After the UK came France, Germany, Sweden, the Netherlands, and Spain. Worldwide, crowdfunding in all its forms

**Table 1:** Evolution 2013–2017.

<table>
<tr><td colspan="5">Gift platforms: (i.e. Bulb in Town, KissKissBankBank, Proarti, Ulule, Commeon, Fosburit, J'adopte un projet, Kocoriko, Freelendease).</td></tr>
<tr><td>Number of projects</td><td>Amount Raised</td><td>Average Amount</td><td>Average Campaign Period</td><td>Success Rate</td></tr>
<tr><td>20105</td><td>94M€</td><td>4, 686€</td><td>32</td><td>44%</td></tr>
<tr><td colspan="5">Lending platforms (i.e. Hellomerci, Unilend, Lendosphere, Lendopolis, PretUp, Prexem Bolden, Blue Bees, Lendix, Les Entrepreneurs, WeShareBonds, Edukys)</td></tr>
<tr><td>Number of projects</td><td>Amount Raised</td><td>Average Amount</td><td>Average Campaign Period</td><td>Success Rate</td></tr>
<tr><td>1515</td><td>202M€</td><td>133,131 €</td><td>15</td><td>18%</td></tr>
<tr><td colspan="5">Equity platforms (i.e. Lumo, Smartangels, Wiseed, HappyCapital, MyNewStartup, Sowefund, IncitFinancement, Raizers, Enerfip, Proximea, Hoodlers, Fundimmo, Booster, Health Investbook, Feedelios, Kiosk To Invest)</td></tr>
<tr><td>Number of projects</td><td>Amount Raised</td><td>Average Amount</td><td>Average Campaign Period</td><td>Success Rate</td></tr>
<tr><td>327</td><td>134M€</td><td>409,173 €</td><td>105</td><td>40%</td></tr>
</table>

Source: BPI.

grew from \$2.6 billion in 2012 to \$34 billion in 2015, shared unequally across continents, with the majority concentrated in North America, Europe and East Asia (Massolution Crowdfunding Industry Report, Crowdsourcing.org 2015). In France specifically, the professional association Crowdfunding France confirm that, between 2015 and 2016, gifting platforms saw a 37% growth in their activities (from €50.1 million to €68.6 raised), while loan platforms grew by 46% (from €66.3 to €96.6 million raised) and investment platforms by 36% (from €50.3 million to €68.6 million).[3] On this basis, crowdfunding is presented as a 'simple', rapid response to the timidity of institutional lenders (not to mention cuts to public funding), and as a profitable solution for investors facing poor returns from 'sovereign' investments (the Livret A, euro life insurance funds, etc.).

While they are supposed to guarantee transparency, the figures given by the platforms should be treated carefully. Any comparison between them is difficult because of the different time periods used to produce them, the criteria and denominations used and each platform's distinctive features. But they do illustrate the capitalist interest of these practices, and give us some indication of the cultural sectors that use them most. Gift platforms with a cultural dimension are the largest in terms of the number of projects submitted. Nevertheless, as the BPI figures compiled between 2013 and 2017 show, in total amounts raised and average sums they are clearly inferior to loan and investment platforms—a gap explained in part by a smaller average total request by project creators, but also by the duration of campaigns, which are longer on investment platforms.

The enthusiasm of the media and politicians should also be tempered somewhat in regard to the real economic significance of crowdfunding, particularly in the cultural field, when we look at the revenues of the sector as a whole (Picard 2018) or compare them to the cumulative totals of existing public funding channels. The figures given here are only indicative, due to the heterogeneity of the criteria used by different European countries and debates about the use of statistics in the cultural domain (Benhamou and Chantepie 2016: 8–18). We may hypothesize that, in certain regards, cultural platforms still offer terrain for experimentation, with a view to expanding and establishing them in other economic sectors—the aim being to ideologically prepare the ground for this propagation, and to minimize the risk involved by encouraging optimal participation among lenders and backers. It is within this optic that many banks have built partnerships with platforms, or created their own, going beyond mere transaction management—for example, committing themselves to participate if funds are successfully raised. La Banque Postale, longstanding partner of KissKissBankBank (and its lending and investment spinoffs), finally acquired the company in June 2017. Contrary to the media and academic discourse that presents crowdfunding as an alternative, we see an increasing integration of these platforms into the existing financial sector. Furthermore, these apparatuses are presented as tools which complement existing sources of credit, something that is reassuring to potential investors and particularly to banking institutions.[4]

## 2. The Importance of Education

Like many other web entrepreneurs, the managers of crowdfunding platforms take on the appearance of educators—evangelists, even—whose mission is to spread their new ideas—their Good News—within communities or social groups that lag behind or are still hostile to this new 'way of the world'. Accordingly, certain platforms have opened training centres, such as Proartischool, the Kickstarter Campus and the Indiegogo Education Centre. The statements of the founders of South African platforms Thundafund and Backabuddy give eloquent examples of their belief in this pedagogical mission: one speaks of 'the spirit of *ubuntu*' and the way in which their platform will be able to 'build on' vernacular systems of collective financing in Africa 'by using a specific tone [...] and using the same jargon, that of community-based care'. His colleague confirms this:

> Yeah, I think again it's education around the tone of the projects. The projects that tend to do well are those that have some sort of a positive

outcome. So of course, because its causes and individuals there's usually crisis-based projects […]. So we've got to help them change the tone […] and often this is a psychology thing, that's my training. To help them and actually take over the wording, campaigning, this is what you do, because otherwise people have quite a sort of negative response. So a lot of the work is really involved in that, in managing all of the campaign creators […]. It really, really takes quite a lot of hand holding.

One of the founders also informed us during the same interview that she drew on her experience of training project creators when authoring two virtual courses on the American education platform Udemy (which also hosts online courses accredited by Kickstarter): 'I use this platform a lot, just in terms of guidance about tone, because they have very strict criteria and I've put two courses online, so I try to transfer this experience to campaigns.' In her doctoral thesis, Marine Jouan writes about her experience as a 'project moderator' with KissKissBankBank, a role that brings together two complementary missions: 'giving advice to project creators and looking for new projects for the platform':

> My work then consisted in 'moderating' requests for fundraising that arrive on the platform [...]. I would also advise them on fundraising. I would show them how to achieve their goal by sending e-mails or getting their family and friends involved. Some project leaders asked for my help during fundraising, worried that the amount raised might stall as the end of the campaign came nearer. I then tried to see with them what they could do in order to achieve the goal they had set. The second part of my work consisted in attracting new projects to the platform, I also did a review of the public and private bodies, associations and organisations that might come into contact with project creators looking for funding. I tried to contact them via e-mail to present the work of KissKissBankBank and invited them to contact us if they were interested. I also made many phone calls to these bodies to ask whether they had any artists in their network who might be interested. I ended up going to some of them to give presentations to interested parties. I responded to their questions about how the platform works and how a fundraising campaign works. (Jouan 2017: 22)

She concludes this brief account of her internal experience with the platform by emphasizing that it offered her the first signs of what she went on to observe in her research—in particular, 'the tensions between the values of mutual aid and the financial dimension, between a generous image of crowdfunding and the realities of fundraising, centred on financial matters'. These values of mutual aid and this generous image seem like a veneer that attempts to dissimulate the true nature of the 'teachings' which these proselytizing managerial discourses proffer to project creators who then, in turn, must repeat the same process among their own little 'crowds'.

Another example is given in the following exchange between two entrepreneurs, reported by Jouan from one of her observations at an internal seminar for the organization Crowdfunding France:

> *Denis*: I really get the feeling that we focus too much on the purely financial side of things, and we forget this whole other aspect of the campaign, and beyond that the project creator of course, and then a community who will contribute a lot of other services apart from funding. It's not just the financial and budgetary aspect. I know we're at Bercy [Ministry of the Economy, Finance and Industry], but other arguments need to be heard, just so that we don't see this as a matter of finance and nothing else […]

> *Lilian*: Once again, I would say yes, you're quite right […]. But at the end of the day, you can say what you want, but crowdfunding is still funding […]. The link between all of this, after all, is that at a some point you get some money. So it's a different way of getting money, but it's still getting money. No one does all of this for nothing! In the end, how do we measure the success of crowdfunding on a site? Either the funds are released or not, depending on what you've put in, and that's the plain fact of the matter. That's why people do it. (Jouan 2017: 148)

The expression 'you can say what you want' refers back to Denis's comment that the values of mutual aid and the construction of 'communities' should be foregrounded, whereas Lilian emphasizes that non-financial support (live capital) and financial support (dead capital) are both ways of obtaining capital. The exchange confirms that the managers of platforms are players, one of whose principal skills consists in being able to 'say what you want' (i.e. their propensity for 'story-telling'). But what is no doubt more interesting is the second part of the quote: 'Either the funds are released or not, depending on what you've put in.' We might relate this comment to the investment of the platform managers who may or may not make a profit when the funds are released, depending on their work in educating project creators. But we may also, of course, relate it to the project creators themselves, who may or may not obtain the funds they asked for (through direct financial or indirect contributions), depending on what they have 'put in', such as labour time in marketing and communication—in short, ideological production as well.

Finally, during an interview with the founder of a crowdfunding site for concerts, we asked to what extent he had to encourage artists to keep their social media pages updated. He responded:

Very much. Especially social media. I've been frustrated at times with the lack of understanding from the music industry of what social media should be […]. I still hammer on constantly when I talk to people about email and I tell them: You've got to be on Facebook, you've got to do what you can on Facebook. Tag people. Go to the private pages, not to your band pages always. And those […] the people that understand that are usually good […]. And it sort of comes back to a question of coaching people at that. We really had to […]. Because again it brings us back to that idea of most artists just want to be artists. They don't want to be marketing people or promotion.

It seems obvious then that a significant proportion of the activity of managers is dedicated to this managerial and psychological guidance, and therefore to forms of production that are entirely ideological. Consequently we may ask to what extent these players, ultimately, are specialized ideological producers, even if this is not exactly the 'heart of their job'. And are they producers of cultural and ideological forms *in just the same way* as the cultural project creators they virtually work with, and whose work they offer to host and to help them propagate? For we must keep in mind that all of this takes place thanks to means of communication that the managers do not necessarily own—even if they may hold shares in these companies and operate in accordance with the wishes of their financial commissioners. Or is the relation between managers and project creators an asymmetrical one, insofar as the ideological production of the former serves objectively to *frame* the latter, in the sense defined by Robert Bihr (1989)—to form and to agitate them? We use the latter term advisedly, in reference to Plekhanov's distinction between propaganda and agitation: the first is the presentation of an important number of generally complex ideas to a small number of people, and the second is the diffusion of a few relatively simple ideas to a mass of people (Plekhanov 1892).

## Conclusion

'Free your creativity!' are the words with which KissKissBankBank welcomes every Internet user to arrive on their website. This tagline is aimed primarily at artists, as an invitation to become project creators, but ultimately it can be read as a leitmotif of the managerial and ideological production of such platforms. In an interview with the newspaper *L'Humanité* on the publication of *The New Spirit of Capitalism*, Luc Boltanski and Ève Chiapello declared: 'We set out from the principle that people are capable by themselves of gauging the gap between what they're told and what they actually experience, so that capitalism somehow has to provide factual reasons to adhere to its discourse. However, the weakness of capitalism is that it all it has to offer is the insatiability of its process of accumulation. Since it is profoundly amoral, it must find outside of itself the motives for engagement, and it is critique that often furnishes these motives.'

In effect, the building and the very functioning of platforms of digital intermediation demand that the different players who use it, aiming to capture economic value, must silently pass over the reality or the 'operationality' of most of the tasks they carry out. The foregrounding of a democratic, innovative, horizontal model (equally prominent in the management discourse of project creators in relation to their 'communities' as in the discursive and procedural management of platforms in relation to 'creative' workers) is an attempt to mask the logics of predation and competition that emerge more clearly as the number of projects grows. By 'projects' here we should understand both the individual fundraising campaigns *and* the *ventures* seeking to claim their share from the windfall of digital intermediation. Cultural crowdfunding platforms are obliged to reassure, to motivate and to mobilize by using a judicious mix of digital technology and marketing techniques (more or less innovative depending on configuration and partners), but in this regard they remain dependent on an ideological production that accounts for a significant proportion of the activities of the various managers. We find the counterpart of this intense work of production of cultural forms (Garnham 1990) among the artistic project creators who, with varying degrees of skill and elegance, improvise appeals to persuade their 'community' of backers to rally behind their project.

The aim of this analysis is not to situate the different forms of labour carried out by and on platforms on a single plane. Rather, it is to suggest some elements which let us compare the tasks which the agents connected by these platforms engage in or submit to—whether those players are managers (or employees with different degrees of responsibility), project creators, or various external 'partners' (primarily funders/donors in the case of crowdfunding campaigns). Each player objectively contributes their time, their capacities and their skills (their live or dead capital) to the general process of production and accumulation.

In fact, here it is not just a question of *the artist as worker*, but also of the mobilization of the artist's 'community'. This also has to contribute to the work of production and communication, as well as making a financial contribution. As with individual startups and incubators, this calls for the development of a 'creative ecosystem', even while attempting to evacuate the question of labour and its remuneration (and therefore its commercialization). Thus we observe the polymorphism of the entrepreneur, a sort of 'matchmaker' at the intersection between players, and between organizations and players, of very disparate origins and influences, whose logics, desires and strategies he must attempt to combine in order to generate economic value. The various facets of their enterprise contribute to the most general development of labour under contemporary capitalism, by participating in what is called, quite incorrectly, the 'collaborative' economy, and by sketching out new 'suggested' modalities perhaps made possible by even greater flexibility, mobility and insecurity.

## Notes

1   http://owni.fr/2010/11/24/mymajorcompany-la-fin-de-lhistoire__Accessed 24 November 2010.
2   https://tousnosprojets.bpifrance.fr/Marche-du-crowdfunding/Actualites/Le-marche-europeen-du-crowdfunding-en-chiffres Accessed 27 February 2019.
3   http://financeparticipative.org/wp-content/uploads/2017/02/Barometre-CrowdFunding-2016.pdf Accessed 5 March 2019.
4   See, for example the article of Stéphane Vromann 'Les banques et les plateformes de crowdfunding sont-elles compatibles?', *les Echos*, 16 December 2016.

## References


Banks, Mark, Rosalind Gill and Stephanie Taylor. 2013. *Theorizing Cultural Work: Labour, Continuity and Change in the Cultural and Creative Industries*. London: Routledge.

Baudoire, Philippe. 2016. *Crowdfunding: mener son projet*. Paris: Arnaud Franel.

Benhamou, Françoise, and Chantepie, Philippe. 2016. Culture et économie: chiffres et cryptes. *Bulletin des bibliothèques de France*, 8, 8–18.

Bénistant, Alix, and Emmanuel Marty (2016). Les médias et le crowdfunding: une analyse des représentations médiatiques, The Conversation, 8 November. Available at: https://theconversation.com/les-medias-et-le-crowdfunding-une-analyse-des-representations-mediatiques-68242.

Bergeron, Henri, Patrick Castel, and Etienne Nouguez. 2013. Éléments pour une sociologie de l'entrepreneur-frontière, *Revue française de sociologie*, 54(2), 263–302.

Bihr, Alan. 1989. *Entre bourgeoisie et prolétariat: l'encadrement capitaliste*. Paris: L'Harmattan.

Bouquillion, Philippe, and Jacob T. Matthews. 2010. *Le Web collaboratif: mutations des industries de la culture et de la communication*. Grenoble: Presses Universitaires de Grenoble.

Boyer, Karine, Alain Chevalier, Jean-Yves Léger, and Aurélie Sannajust, *Le Crowdfunding*. Paris: La Découverte, 2016.

Brabham, Daren. C. 2009. Crowdsourcing the Public Participation Process for Planning Projects, *Planning Theory*, 8(3), 242–262.

Cardon, Dominique, and Antonio A. Cassilli. 2015. *Qu'est ce que le Digital Labor?* Paris: Ina Éditions.

Céré, Joël, Yannig Roth and François Pétavy. 2015. The State of Crowdsourcing in 2015: How the World's Biggest Brands and Companies are Opening Up to Consumer Creativity, Eyeka Analyst Report.

Collin, Pierre, and Nicolas Colin. 2013. Mission d'expertise sur la fiscalité de l'économie numérique, French Ministry of Finance and Economy report.

Crowdsourcing.org 2015. Massolution 2015 CF: The Crowdfunding Industry Report. (See: http://reports.crowdsourcing.org.)

Deleuze, Gilles. 1995. Postscript on Control Societies, in *Negotiations, 1972–1990*, trans. by M. Joughin. New York: Columbia University Press, pp.177–182.

De Stefano, Valerio. 2016. The Rise of the 'Just-in-time Workforce': On-demand Work, Crowdwork and Labour Protection in the 'Gig-economy.' *Conditions of Work and Employment Series* No. 71. International Labour Office, Inclusive Labour Markets, Labour Relations and Working Conditions Branch, Geneva.

Divard, Ronan. 2013. La participation des consommateurs aux campagnes publicitaires : ses formes, ses avantages et ses limites, *Gestion*, 38(4), 61–73.

Dujarier, Marie-Anne. 2014. *Le Travail du consommateur, de McDo à eBay: comment nous coproduisons ce que nous achetons.* Paris: La Découverte.

Epstein, Michael J. 2018. *Crowdfunding Basics in 30 Minutes: How to Use Kickstarter, Indiegogo, and Other Crowdfunding Platforms to Support Your Entrepreneurial and Creative Dreams.* i30 Media Corporation.

Flichy, Patrice. 2017. *Les Nouvelles Frontières du travail à l'ère numérique.* Paris: Seuil.

Fohr, Robert. 2016. Le Crowdfunding, une nouvelle forme de démocratisation culturelle?, in *Le Crowdfunding culturel*, ed. by Anaïs Del Bono and Guillaume Maréchal. Librinova.

Freedman, David M., and Matthew R. Nutting. 2015. A Brief History of Crowdfunding Including Rewards, Donation, Debt, and Equity Platforms in the USA, <http://www.freedman-chicago.com/ec4i/History-of-Crowdfunding.pdf> [accessed 27 February 2019].

Fuchs, Christian. 2014. *Digital Labour and Karl Marx.* London and New York: Routledge.

Garnham, Nicholas. 1990. *Capitalism and Communication: Global Culture and the Economics of Information.* London: Sage.

Gayoso, Émile. 2015. Les plateformes de co-innovation, *Réseaux*, 2, 121–149.

Gille, Laurent. 1997. L'Impact des technologies d'information dans la production de marchés. Paris: Sirius.

Graham, Mark, Isis Hjorth, and Vili Lehdonvirta. 2017. Digital Labour and Development Impacts of Global Digital Labour Platforms and the Gig Economy on Worker Livelihoods. *Transfer: European Review of Labour and Research* 28(1): 35–62

Hendrickx, Marianne. 2014. *Crowdfunding: Mode d'emploi.* Liège: Edipro.

Hesmondhalgh, David. 2008. Cultural and Creative Industries, in *The Sage Handbook of Cultural Analysis*, ed. by Tony Bennett and John Frow. London: Sage.

Hesmondhalgh, David and Sarah Baker. 2011. *Creative Labour: Media Work in Three Cultural Industries*. London: Routledge.

Huws, Ursula. 2003. *The Making of a Cybertariat: Virtual Work in a Real World*. New York: Monthly Review Press.

———. 2014. *Labor in the Global Digital Economy: The Cybertariat Comes of Age*. New York: Monthly Review Press.

Iizuka, Marianne. 2015. *Le Crowdfunding: les rouages du crowdfunding*. Paris: Edubanque.

Jaillet-Roman, Marie-Christine. 2002. De la Généralisation de l'injonction au projet, *Empan*, 45(1), 19–24.

Jenkins, Henry. 2006. *Convergence Culture: Where Old and New Media Collide*. New York and London: New York University Press.

Jouan, Marine. 2017. *La Construction sociale du marché du crowdfunding en France* (doctoral dissertation) Telecom ParisTech.

Katz, Elihu, and Paul L. Lazarsfeld. 2017 [1955]. *Personal Influence: The Part Played by People in the Flow of Mass Communications*. New York: Routledge.

Kenney, Martin, and John Zysman. 2016. What is the Future of Work? Understanding the Platform Economy and Computation-intensive Automation.Berkeley Roundtable on the International Economy. Proto-paper prepared for Radcliffe Institute, Conference on Work and Welfare in the Platform Economy. Avaiable at https://brie.berkeley.edu/sites/default/files/briewp-2016–9.pdf [last accessed 27 February 2019].

Kuppuswamy, Venkat, and B.L. Bayus. 2013. *Crowdfunding Creative Ideas: The Dynamics of Project Backers in Kickstarter* <https://papers.ssrn.com/sol3/papers.cfm?abstract_id=2234765http://business.illinois.edu/ba/seminars/2013/Spring/bayus_paper.pdf> [accessed 27 February 2019].

Lebraty, Jean-Fabrice, and Katia Lobre-Lebraty. 2015. *Crowdsourcing: porté par le foule*. London: ISTE Editions.

Lemoine, Phillipe. 2014. La Nouvelle Grammaire du succès: la transformation numérique de l'économie française. Report to the French Government.

Mairesse, François. 2016. Les Modèles participatifs dans les musées, in *Crowdfunding, industries culturelles et démarche participative*, ed. by Laurent Creton and Kira Kitsopanidou. Bern: Peter Lang, 99–113.

Matthews, Jacob, Vincent Rouzé and Jérémy Vachet. 2014. *La Culture par les foules? Le Crowdfunding en question*. Paris: MKF Editions.

Menger, Pierre-Michel. 2002. *Portrait de l'artiste en travailleur: métamorphoses du capitalisme*. Paris: Le Seuil.

Miège, Bernard. 2000. *Les Industries du contenu face à l'ordre informationnel*. Grenoble: Presses Universitaires de Grenoble.

Nixon, Bruce. 2014. Toward a Political Economy of 'Audience Labour' in the Digital Era, *Triple C*, 12(2), 713–734.

Picard, Tristan. 2018. *Le poids économique direct de la culture en 2016*. Paris: DEPS.

Plekhanov, Georgi. 1892. *On the Tasks of the Socialists in the Russian Famine.* Geneva.

Renault, Sophie. 2014. Crowdsourcing: la nébuleuse des frontières de l'organisation et du travail, *Revue interdisciplinaire management, homme & entreprise*, 2(11), 23–40.

Ricordeau, Vincent. 2013. *Crowdfunding: le crowdfunding bouscule l'économie!* Paris: FYP éditions.

Scholz, Trebor, ed. 2012. *Digital Labor: The Internet as Playground and Factory.* London and New York: Routledge.

Smith, Rebecca, and Sarah Leberstein. 2015. Rights on Demand: Ensuring Workspace Standards and Worker Security in the on-demand Economy National Employment Law Project. www.nelp.org.

Simonet, Maud. 2010. *Le Travail bénévole: engagement citoyen ou travail gratuit?* Paris: La Dispute.

Smyrnaios, Nikos. 2017. *Les Gafam contre l'internet.* Paris: INA Éditions.

Stegmaier, Jamey. 2015. *A Crowdfunder's Strategy Guide: Build a Better Business by Building Community.* Oakland, CA: Berrett-Koehler.

Surowiecki, James. 2004. *The Wisdom of Crowds.* New York: Anchor.

Terranova, Tiziana. 2000. Free Labor: Producing Culture for the Digital Economy, *Social Text*, 18(2), 33–58.

Vercellone, Carlo. 2008. La Thèse du capitalisme cognitif: une mise en perspective historique et théorique in *Les Nouveaux Horizons du capitalisme: Pouvoirs, valeurs, temps*, ed. by Gabriel Colletis and Bernard Paulré. Paris: Economica, pp. 71–95.

# CHAPTER 5

# Globalization and the Logics of Capitalism

Jacob Matthews, Stéphane Costantini and Alix Bénistant

This chapter focuses on the development of crowdfunding platforms in sub-Saharan Africa and Latin America, considering this phenomenon from the point of view of a twofold hypothesis: that it participates in the extension towards the South of the market logics that have driven the emergence of digital intermediation platforms in the West, and that it may be an opportunity for hybridisation and fruitful social and cultural alternatives. Indeed, the fundamental question which initially guided our investigations was as follows, two-fold: To what extent is the emergence of crowdfunding in these countries characterized by the replication of the dominant logics which we have analysed in the previous three chapters, and which are characterized as we have seen, on the one hand, by the remanence (and in many respects) an intensification of the capitalist logics at play in the field of communication and culture industries, and on the other hand, by the development of an ideology of collaboration and participation that appears to be particularly effective with regard to relations of production and labour conditions? Or, can we observe specific trends and phenomena pertaining specifically to the local/regional or endogenous economic, social and cultural configurations, which might in turn support the emergence and development of hitherto unseen tools for social development

---

**How to cite this book chapter:**
Matthews, J., Costantini, S. and Bénistant, A. 2019. Globalization and the Logics of Capitalism. In: Rouzé, V. (ed.) *Cultural Crowdfunding: Platform Capitalism, Labour and Globalization*. Pp. 79–98. London: University of Westminster Press. DOI: https://doi.org/10.16997/book38.e. License: CC-BY-NC-ND 4.0

and the authentic diversification of cultural exchanges and flows – in particular platforms inspired either by emancipatory and post-colonial political movements or by vernacular structures of mutual assistance?

## Introductory Remarks

This chapter contains four sections. The first one develops several introductory remarks, taking into account the specificities of the research contexts in comparison with those covered in the previous chapters. The second gives a brief survey of the different categories of players present in the field of crowdfunding (and particularly crowdfunding for cultural production), and their distinctive strategies and logics. The third provides a clearer understanding of the discourses produced and/or propagated by the players involved in crowdfunding and its potential development. The last section addresses a specific aspect of the discourse and practice of the players in crowdfunding: efforts at 'pedagogy' and 'education' aimed at local populations.

As a first introductory remark, let us state that, in line with Christiaan de Beukelaer (2015), we have not limited our analysis to cultural productions (contents or services) resulting from the productive activity of the cultural and communications industries. Like de Beukelaer, we have broadened our focus to include cultural expressions that are the product of activities that may not necessarily be understood as a part of the sectors or production cycles associated with these industries. We have also taken into consideration the question of the informal economy: given its importance in sub-Saharan Africa, and in certain Latin American countries, we must understand it not as a problem but as a component of cultural industries as they emerge and develop in the South. A question then arises: does the development of platforms for collaborative production and financing contribute to the formalization of this economy? Or are informal modes of production and value creation instead perpetuated on such platforms, presenting hybrid or even alternative models to Western norms?

A second introductory clarification bears upon the problematic of the flows of culture and ideology between North and South. De Beukelaer emphasizes that, when the development of so-called 'creative' industries is presented as a vector for the realization of 'cultural potential' in the countries of the South, a subliminal neoliberal discourse becomes overt (De Beukelaer 2015: 79). He continues:

> The discourse of the creative economy is contrarily colonizing the cultural imagery, primarily through the perceived orthodoxy of the conditions for creation and circulation, rather than through the influx of cultural expressions, which is crucial in the cultural imperialism thesis. (De Beukelaer 2015: 129)

It seemed important to us to assess this argument. We might ask whether the cultural imperialism of our times resides less in the superficial messages of 'content' than in those vaster and simultaneously more effective cultural forms that are the ideological 'grand discourses' of collaboration, creativity, sustainable development, diversity, empowerment, and so on. We have therefore tried to verify how far the development of these apparatuses is accompanied by the production or dissemination of 'grand discourses'.

Nevertheless—this is our third point—we set out from the principle that social financing (like other uses of digital intermediation platforms) can also be used within the framework of vernacular or autonomous cultural expressions that self-identify as resistant or alternative—in relation to either authoritarian or semi-authoritarian political regimes, or ideological and socioeconomic logics imported from the Western North, including the discourses and practices of the 'creative' economy. In parallel, we should recall that, contrary to the Western configuration, much cultural production in Africa (and in the Andean countries) falls outside of any appropriation through intellectual property rights, which are the cornerstone of the 'creative' industries. This historical process of the 'enclosure' of culture by intellectual property (Nixon 2014) remains incomplete in the countries of the South, and has met with tenacious resistance movements, which make for interesting cases of the incarnation of the commons within the cultural field (Lobato 2010). These regions may potentially offer prefigurations of postcapitalist forms of organization, free of the asymmetrical power relations characteristic of Western 'collaborative' apparatuses. We have kept this hypothesis in mind in our empirical research. But we have also been attentive to evidence which confirms the inverse hypothesis: that the Global South is ahead of the old Western societies, but this time as the 'avant-garde of the market epoch' (Comaroff and Comaroff 2012)—a distinction due especially to the absence of labour regulations, permitting a wholesale 'uberization' of the relations of production.

A final introductory observation involves vernacular crowdfunding systems in these regions (including *tontine, iquib, pasanku,* and *susu*) and their distant cousin, the international monetary and financial system. In the interview extract below, the co-founder of the South African platform Backabuddy mentions traditional devices of community solidarity and mutual aid, while emphasizing the platform's dependency on financial flows from the North:

> In African culture, there has always been a spirit of *ubuntu* which, while based on mutual aid within the community, has never yet been translated into the form of charitable giving—which leaves us still largely dependent on external sources for fundraising.

These statements raise wider issues than that of cultural production in itself. Using cultural crowdfunding as one of his examples, de Beukelaer emphasizes that the expansion of digital technology incontestably brings about possibilities that were previously unimaginable. As he remarks, though, the emergence of intermediation platforms in this domain has taken place mostly within the framework of partnerships with Western economic players (as well as foreign governmental agencies and international organizations), and has generally profited international markets (De Beukelaer 2015: 89). Studying cultural crowdfunding leads us to the question of the presence of Western economic (and political) players in sub-Saharan Africa, in particular, and their control or influence over financial flows, policies (social, cultural and land use planning), and modes of labour organization (cultural or otherwise). On a macroeconomic level, the economist Costas Lapavitsas notes that, 'during the 2000s, capital has flowed from poor to rich countries on a large scale … Even impoverished Africa contributed to the net flow of capital from poor to rich countries' (Lapavitsas 2009: 118). Lapavitsas shows how this process was largely driven by the expansion of Western banks into developing countries over the course of the same period: 'Significant proportions of total banking assets are now foreign-owned even in low income countries, most notably in Africa where foreign ownership constitutes more than two thirds of banking assets in ten countries' (Lapavitsas 2009: 122). In the context of our research this question became unavoidable, insofar as cultural crowdfunding (and, by extension, the crowdfunding of 'technological' and 'entrepreneurial' projects) seems in many regards like a Trojan horse for significant developments in fintech.

In summary, our fundamental question is as follows: to what extent is the emergence of crowdfunding in these countries characterized by the replication of dominant Western logics or, on the contrary, by hybridizations and unforeseen alternatives? This chapter contains three sections which offer some responses to this question. The first gives a brief survey of the different categories of players present in the field of crowdfunding (and particularly crowdfunding for cultural production), and their distinctive strategies and logics. The second provides a clearer understanding of the discourses produced and/or propagated by the players involved in crowdfunding and its potential development. The third section addresses a specific aspect of the discourse and practice of the players in crowdfunding: efforts at 'pedagogy' and 'education' aimed at local populations.


## The Different Categories of Players Present in the Regions

A survey of cultural crowdfunding in Latin America and sub-Saharan Africa allows us, firstly, to identify a category of endogenous actors. The most emblematic representatives of these are the South Africa-based Thundafund, which remains financially independent, and Ideame, the principal Latin American actor, which is now established in seven countries, including the US. This platform claims to be a regional replica of the American model, while affirming its specificity by espousing a form of local legitimacy: it presents itself as a

Latin American platform for Latin Americans, including those living in the US (demonstrated especially by the 'Create Miami' campaign). There are other endogenous platforms in the region—in Brazil, for example, which occupies a distinctive position in the south of the continent, especially because of its language, and celebrates this distinction beyond the language itself through a refusal of the North American model. Brazil is home to companies like Catarse, Kickante and Queremos, which was later adapted to the US under the name Wedemand—with $900,000 in support from an English investment fund, Talis Capital. Most endogenous Latin American platforms were launched using their own money, often that of their founders, who are mainly urban youth from the upper 5% of the population. The endogenous platforms with the greatest growth are those specializing in loans, such as Afluenta in Argentina and Kubo Financiero in Mexico. (When we interviewed the latter's CEO, it was the only platform to be regulated, holding a bank licence granted by the government; a law has since been passed modelled on the US Jobs Act.) These are also the platforms most exposed (and disposed) to foreign investment—particularly American capital, which counts on and shares in their rapid growth.

Endogenous platforms have also emerged in West Africa. But their level of activity remains low, and they too are being supported by large Western companies or banks like Société Générale, which has developed incubators and various other projects in the region, often in partnership with national public agencies and international organizations. Almost all these initiatives stem from the wider emergence of fintech and its players—either banks and banking-related (Waalam is a secondary spinoff of a financial assets consultancy), or telecoms and telecom-related (Orange, Paydunya, Intouch). Crowdfunding is seen as a set of services that can be offered to users, but whose 'value added' remains to be proven—something evident in an interview with an executive at Orange:

> We're looking at crowdfunding tools. Through the Orange Digital Venture fund, Orange has invested in a player that is the French and European leader, KissKissBankBank, which has three types of sites [...] and obviously they have some interest in Africa, which is currently looking at everything that is emerging right now. No one knows the truth in this area, and we don't have a clear idea of the dynamics of the market, what the uptake will be [...]. We're going to launch the first platforms, and what interests us is the lessons we can learn from the experience.

We encounter both a keen interest and a wait-and-see attitude on the part of Western players in crowdfunding, with large conglomerates moving their pawns and cautiously observing the developments and experiments that are underway. We find the same slow wait-and-see attitude on the part of national economic players, as illustrated by an interview with a representative of Intouch, a 'mobile money' aggregator solution, working on a white label basis for the

French conglomerate Total. Numerous players are focusing on this area, and it seems crowdfunding is currently being approached through this prism (for example, by sending premium SMSs). Answering a question about the risks of direct competition with European and North American players, in the case where a platform such as Kickstarter allies itself with Intouch to launch a service specific to West Africa, the Intouch representative responded:

> We need patient players who have already tested certain models. And it will be difficult to avoid international players—in fact, they are already readying themselves for Africa. You wonder who will dare take the first step, even if we have seen some preparing to do so, but we'll see what comes of it.

For all these reasons, it is difficult to consider these players as properly endogenous, and one should emphasize that development is still low compared with the situation in the North and in East Asia. This is particularly the case for many of the countries where we carried out fieldwork, such as Ethiopia and Burkina Faso, where at the time of writing no endogenous crowdfunding platform had emerged and almost all fundraising campaigns have been realized through Western players, generally by soliciting contributions from people living in the countries of the North, including diaspora communities. This comparatively low level of development is partly a matter of Internet penetration and the technical resources available to local populations, even though the use of mobile telephones and collective computer stations has grown sharply over the last fifteen years. The limits of social financing in sub-Saharan Africa and some Latin American countries are also related to the low usage of banks by local populations (10 to 15% of the population in Senegal, for example), and to the fact that, until now, crowdfunding has been the province of economic players (contributors, large groups and platforms) based principally in the West. We do, however, observe certain adaptation strategies by platforms, or strategies of circumvention by project creators. (In Africa, these strategies include building links with 'mobile money' applications and encouraging users to contribute directly. In Latin America, they include the use of MiCochinito, which enables cash payments in local shops.)

Hence, we observe a substantial number of players from the North interested in crowdfunding in various ways, beginning with the two major US platforms, Kickstarter and Indiegogo, for funding local projects. This includes South Africa, where Thundafund, Backabuddy and Jumpstarter nevertheless strive to compete with the US offer by highlighting their supposed proximity to project creators and contributors. In Latin America, we also see a substantial number of exogenous players, along with an apparent retreat on the part of financing players from the North in terms of participation in local companies: it very much seems as if they are waiting for the market to crystallize around a small number of players in order to work out how to invest or what acquisitions to make. There is also a significant local implantation of North American players in Latin America. Kickstarter is the most present: according to Sebastian Di Lullo, CEO of Ideame, it alone is responsible for half the total amount raised by all Latin American players in 2016–17. Ideame also pursues a strategy of purchasing national players and opening offices in different countries in the hope of attracting different categories of the population—particularly the most wealthy and those who see themselves as being part of a 'creative class'. We therefore observe a domination characterized both by the consolidation of a number of players present over the whole territory and by pressure from the most powerful players on the international level. This twofold domination is on the one hand a brake on the emergence of local players (numerous platforms have closed or are barely surviving in various Latin American countries, including KapitalZocial in Peru or La Chèvre in Colombia) and on the other hand manifests itself in the normalization and standardization of these apparatuses on the North American model. Although the expansion strategy of Thundafund, for example, is more limited, these remarks generally hold for sub-Saharan Africa, but with one caveat: the presence of large players from the North seems to go hand in hand with the emergence of seemingly endogenous players, whose crowdfunding platforms constitute only one element in a wider palette of mobile services.

## A Diversity of Players, a Repertoire of Common Discourses

### 1. Project Creators and Endogenous Cultural Workers

Predictably, our interviews with potential or actual project creators have generally been marked by their overt enthusiasm, summed up by Gaissiri Dia, founder of the platform Waalam: 'I have confidence in the next generation to take the initiative, they will grasp the opportunities that are beneficial for us'. Emphasis is placed on a supposed 'entrepreneurial culture' in sub-Saharan Africa, and to a lesser extent in Latin America. The discourses of many project creators frequently express a desire to contribute to alternative forms of social financing that lie off the beaten track of Western platforms. Despite a reminder of the pitfalls, Heinz Winckler, a South African musician who funded the production of an album through Thundafund, displayed such enthusiasm when we interviewed him about the challenges faced by social financing in his country:

> I think it's the lack of knowledge of the general public of what it is exactly, of what it means, so there's just a, there are some kind of education needed in a way, for people to understand [...] it's mainly knowing what it is, how it works, you know, that it's worked before, you can trust it, you will get what you paid for and it must be easier, it must be easy to work

with. And I think it sounds like Thunderfund have sorted that out so, you know, hope […]. I'm sure they'll get better.

In Senegal and Burkina Faso we interviewed a number of musicians who had used platforms based in France (Ulule, KissKissBankBank) to finance the production of albums aiming at niche 'world music' markets. In these cases, the campaigns had been successful because the artists already had a 'market in France'. One interviewee in Senegal explained the success of such campaigns (and, in contrast, the limits of crowdfunding for cultural projects on potential national or pan-African platforms):

> It isn't something we'd be afraid of doing, but it's just that it may be a bit early for it. In any case, I see artists trying to do something on Facebook because it's true that it the sector is a little neglected. In France it's different, artists like Grégoire are crowdfunded, but here people don't take the risk because money is complicated here. People don't talk about it, they are incapable of defining what they expect to make.

This is an interesting remark, invoking one of the 'mythical figures' of crowdfunding, Grégoire: the success of that particular campaign (and the 'expectations' in terms of the funds that could be raised) had been carefully prepared and orchestrated by the platform MyMajorCompany well ahead of its launch, in particular by signing a publishing contract beforehand with the distributor Warner Music France. Not that this matters: the same myth of quasi-organic crowdfunding in the West, which will inevitably 'trickle down' to the South, is expressed by Ken Aicha Sy (a member of the collective Wakh'Art, which led a fruitful crowdfunding campaign). He unhesitatingly places music production, healthcare application development, and a very specific context of work organization on the same plane:

> Especially in music, there are so many artists who use these sites to fund foreign tours and records, those who have a following abroad ask their audience for help. I think it's because there is a demand that young people develop a distinctive offer, and then the more that offer is developed, the more it will be suited to people's needs. For example, I've met people who make applications for healthcare here in Senegal, I know social entrepreneurs in the prison system who use it to enable their work with prisoners. Once the platforms exist, demand will grow, and today we're a country with 8 million people connected to the Internet, there are 14 million Senegalese, so it's a big market.

Alongside these positively motivated users of the platforms, we also met numerous cultural workers who seemed overcome by the obstacles they met when setting up a social financing campaign. They were often eager to get started and already users of networks for information and computer technology, but were held back either by the everyday business of 'survival' or by other time-consuming and financially indispensable work. This is the case of an Ethiopian engineer, Getnet Aseffa, the founder of IcogLabs. He launched an unsuccessful campaign on Indiegogo to finance an educational project involving artificial intelligence. According to him, the attempt failed principally because he lacked the time necessary for preparing and promoting the campaign, since he was busy with accounting and financial data management tasks outsourced to his 'laboratory' by Australian companies. Here the limitations of the enthusiastic discourses become quite clear: stories of successful project creators are the exception, and campaigns are marked by vicissitudes and obstacles that were underestimated at the outset. The Afrikaner protest musician Koos Kombuis emphasizes this, based on his experience with Jumpstarter:

> You don't count the sleepless nights. Like, I heard only after I'd signed up that I need a launch video, so you've got to find a professional person to take a decent video. That costs money [...]. Getting everyone together, for this, it was a headache you know, because when you put [...] the record label, I mean it's horrible, but they do everything for you. You don't have to think […]. It took a whole year, I mean I researched it, starting thinking about it, getting the CD done, it was like a year of my life that I don't want, I had one year, one week holiday last year that I took off with my family. It was the most exhausting year of my life. So I wouldn't do it again. But I'm not dissatisfied, I'm a happy customer, I believe in crowdfunding.

### 2. *Platform Managers and Other Endogenous Entrepreneurs*

Among those who work for local platforms (or those that belong to the 'ecosystem' of digital technologies and mobile money) we find a similar zealotry, tempered with a certain realism about the constraints that are slowing down the development of social financing, especially in sub-Saharan Africa. Christian Palouki, CTO of the payment solutions aggregator Paydunya, offers an example of this wishful thinking. He envisions a future where the population may still not have fully adopted bank account usage as in the West, but where mobile money devices will play an analogous role:

> It's this habit of paying with cash that slows everything down here in Africa […]. People are afraid of paying on the Internet and it slows everything down. They are afraid they won't receive what they've paid for, or they're afraid someone will steal their data. What would be interesting for us would be to succeed in convincing people that there are structures in place, and that's what we're working on. We are looking for innovative means of payment so as to achieve what is called financial inclusion.

Yet to our eyes this seems to be more like a specific way of developing and legitimating services that are an integral part of the informal economy. Here again, as with other 'mobile money' services, what is being sought is not so much a formalization of the economy as an adaptation to its informal character so as to render it productive (financially, at least).

Latin American endogenous players seem somewhat more ready to express their reservations about the perceived risks of universalizing Western-style crowdfunding. Rodrigo Maia, founder of the Brazilian platform Catarse, is wary of the standardization of project pages that he sees underway in a number of his competitors on the continent:

> They produce the page for the project creators. Which isn't good because, when you do that, you sever the link with the reality of the campaign, and you sell something that isn't authentic [...]. Of course, no doubt you've seen that there are companies in the US that now offer to produce crowdfunding campaigns as a service. That's because the ecosystem is already burgeoning and moving in other directions. Here, we have to support [authentic] behaviours and make them accessible to the people.

Paradoxically, the strategies of these players may end up consolidating the Western, 'entrepreneurial', fundamentally pro-capitalist discourse, and in particular the version of it that promotes the 'sharing economy' and forms of deregulated labour through digital intermediation platforms (Scholz 2017). We can see the limits of positioning oneself as 'alternative' when this player justifies the growing precariousness of his own platform's workers:

> We don't have trainees who work for nothing, but nevertheless we don't pay people what they deserve [...]. We're not proud of it, but I don't know whether crowdfunding or any other kind of initiative or attempt at innovation would be possible without this kind of arrangement between the workforce and the founders.

The local players interested in social financing we met in Ethiopia set out a similar vision of innovation, one dependent on the flexibility and precariousness of workers. Semina Hadera, owner of a marketing company who became involved in crowdfunding a photography book, described recruiting helpers on Facebook: 'Social media allows the effective and inexpensive promotion of your work [...]. If you use it strategically, it works.'

Other singular configurations in terms of the management of internal labour of platforms were indicated to us—for instance, the two sister platforms Thundafund and Backabuddy. Both are based in South Africa, but fully integrated into international financial flows. This sometimes proves paradoxically counterproductive:

> With Thundafund we did initially have our dev partners in Bulgaria,
> that's where the actual programs were based. What we realized over
> here, was, and actually our initial tech partners were based in the UK,
> and the dev team in Bulgaria [...]. But we discovered that having your
> tech partners in another country, while it made financial sense it was a
> nightmare when it came to cultural and social differences. What I mean
> by that is they run on an Orthodox Christian calendar, and we run on
> the Western Christian calendar—Easter happens this weekend, Easter
> happens that weekend. We're on holiday, they're on holiday. Thirty holi-
> days, 30 days of holiday in South Africa, 30 days holiday in Bulgaria—
> 60 days in which neither of us can actually work. You just don't think of
> that stuff, well we didn't, so it became an absolute nightmare.

Other local players turn to complementary service offerings, confirming the
results of our research into the uses of crowdfunding in Europe and North
America. Whether in the case of project creators or platform entrepreneurs,
numerous examples show how fundraising becomes a pretext for (or a prel-
ude to) other activities, like marketing or brokering. As an example, Gerhard
Maree, founder of Citysoirée, a South African social financing site for private
concerts, reoriented his offerings toward consultancy and services such as
audience profiling, marketing, and ticket management for shows organized by
third parties via the platform: 'I think Citysoirée's brand as a creative entity has
become more valuable than as a crowdfunding platform.'

### 3. Exogenous Players and International Organizations

Within the context of our research we have been confronted by the importance
of very active exogenous stakeholders seeking to create 'inclusive' dynamics in
the interests of large industrial or financial groups or that of the economic pow-
ers they represent and assist (in particular the embassies of major Western pow-
ers). In West Africa, this type of process is typically encouraged by international
organizations like the United Nations Program for Development (UNPD), as
well as by supranational financial bodies like InfoDev[1] and the World Bank,
WAEMU[2], and CBWAS[3]. In our research we were able to interview at length
a representative of the French company Orange who was in charge of developing digital economy initiatives in West Africa. Having pointed out that he
was not 'a great expert in development aid'—which he argues is fundamentally
counterproductive—he explained Orange's general approach, which consists in
'contributing to endogenous development' by developing 'an SME ecosystem
using digital technologies'. To this end, the group deploys a long term strategy
that will most likely be unprofitable in the early stages, 'opening local funds, on
a per-country basis, run locally by local teams': 'the aim of those who invest in

these vehicles is not to make money, or to lose it, but above all to consolidate the stronger SMEs and guide them toward better instruments that are a little larger and more profitable.' Careful to make it known that these funds operate 'autonomously', he clarifies:

> We didn't want to put Orange solutions in place, because it's not necessarily our speciality, we don't necessarily have the skills, and we wanted to establish structures that have legitimacy. We can't legitimately do the work of banks, do guidance work, make up for all the deficiencies around us. On the other hand, we can legitimately go and meet with certain players in the public sector, the private sector, the civil sector, and get together and set up projects.

As we can see, there is a good deal of careful wording in this discourse. It is a matter of Orange's 'legitimacy' to intervene economically in these former French colonies alongside partners as illustrious as Total and African states. The supposed aim is to enable the financing of local SMEs, including in the domain of crowdfunding. To back up the idea that this is a matter of 'local bodies, directed and run locally for local bodies' or 'true tools of endogenous development', the Orange representative insisted that:

> If we create a cultural incubator, on the board we're going to have the minister of culture, that's how it goes—and then we'll go look for people who can put a bit of money on the table, without it being too much of a problem for them, so as to bring to life a space that will make a structural contribution in the cultural domain. And it will do its work with a degree of independence, because it is an intersection between these different people and has to manage relations between different stakeholders and organize its work for the benefit of the cultural domain. [...] This empowers the local players who will do the work.

This is a significant example, not only insofar as this type of body is effectively being called upon to construct an 'ecosystem' in which the budding platforms will eventually participate, but also because in it we find the very principles that lie at the basis of the activity of intermediation Marine Jouan describes, referring to the notion of 'border-entrepreneur' which was evoked in the previous chapter (Jouan 2017: 335). In this type of structural initiative we can see at work both the transference of a discourse of 'empowerment' and the implementation of mechanisms that clearly restrain the supposed autonomy of endogenous entrepreneurs.

If the forms of intervention are more discreet in Latin America, they are certainly not absent, as shown by the growing importance of liberally-oriented public policies which encourage 'individual responsibility', inspired by the great Western discourses. In April 2016, FOMIN—or Multilateral Investment

Fund, created in 1993 to promote the development of the private sector in Latin America and administered by the Inter-American Development Bank based in New York—released a report, *Economia colaborativa en América latina*. This gives a good illustration of this process, as does the US's readiness to support this type of development, which is centred on a 'creative economy' in which the state plays less of a part, and which sees the individual-entrepreneur as the creator of wealth and the vector of growth.

In addition, we must recognize that the endogenous players we met emphasized the use—or even necessity—of this kind of partnership. Representatives of the African Crowdfunding Association (ACfA) told us:

> Our objective for 2017 is to exert pressure on a number of agencies with which we are in contact, notably international ones, for whom South Africa is not a priority. They tell us they are interested if we initiate projects in West Africa or East Africa. There is the CIPE. There is also the Agence Française de Développement.

The AFD is well known in France. The CIPE (Centre for Individual Private Enterprise) is less so: it is one of the four central institutes of the National Endowment for Democracy, a 'non-profit' spinoff of the US Chamber of Commerce.

### 4. National Public Players

Finally, our research in different regions of Latin America and Africa has enabled us to collect some revealing evidence on the discourses that accompany national and local policies directed toward the different players involved in crowdfunding, although it would be difficult to draw any unified conclusion from them. Two major trends are however evident, ranging from a relative avoidance or misunderstanding of the question to an apparent desire to place it in the most general register of the neoliberal transformation of public policy, driven in particular by the international organizations and major Western players mentioned above.

In Ethiopia, and in South Africa to a lesser extent, we observed a certain bewilderment on the part of public officials we met. This was confirmed, among others, by Lunda Wright, a representative of the ACfA:

> When public institutions want to establish partnerships with us, they come with a preconception of what crowdfunding is, based on how they see Kickstarter and Indiegogo. Some have understood that there are contextual factors, and that we therefore have to take local platforms into consideration, but others are stuck in this idea that we have to work with the big Western platforms. And they treat local platforms with a degree of mistrust.

This has not however prevented the central government from supporting and funding a training programme on the use of social financing platforms, as discussed in the next section. In response to our question about support for projects that may benefit from social financing, a representative of the Ethiopian tourism ministry (which is responsible for culture) mentioned two businesses that export craft goods to the North American and European markets, one financed by the World Bank, the other by bilateral agreements under the aegis of UNESCO. But he noted that, unfortunately, once this support ended such activity would decline through a 'lack of strategy' on the part of the cultural producers. By his own admission, an absence of any coordinated policy in this domain has resulted from a lack of statistics and applicable indicators on cultural production: 'Without that, we can't produce data to connect to other economic indicators', he told us, avoiding the question. This elliptical response shows how little interest such issues still provoke in most sub-Saharan African countries. In Senegal, the position of political decision makers remains just as confused, despite the optimism of one of our interviewees, the entrepreneur Christian Palouki:

> The Senegalese state has begun to get involved in the digital and the cultural sector. They have launched a program called PSE (Plan Sénégal Émergent) whose objective is to allow Senegal to enter the digital era. They're currently developing various mechanisms that will allow us to develop digital, to get us on board.

In Latin America, the discourse of political decision-makers is also marked by a certain enthusiasm, and in certain cases is based on public policies of support or legitimation, recognizing for example that the region is 'fertile soil for the implantation of crowdfunding, since systems of community and collaborative financing already exist', as suggested in the report *Economia colaborativa en América latina* mentioned above. Thus, we see local and national initiatives to extend the practice toward less well-off segments of the population: Argentina's 'mercado de industrias creativas' (MICA–'creative industries market') programme, which uses public support to help potential and current project creators; the 'día del crowdfunding' ('crowdfunding day') in Mexico; and the 'semana del crowdfunding' ('crowdfunding week') in Chile which, in particular, has provided training for project leaders in partnership with the platform Ideame. All of these initiatives are characterized by a marked political desire to leave behind the 'European' style public management of cultural financing, instead making space for individual initiatives. Paradoxically, we observe a displacement (also seen in Europe) of public funds towards events that supposedly herald the aforementioned 'creative economy', with the aim of avoiding a model felt to be too top-down, and at the same time we observe a prominent discourse advocating the greater autonomy and responsibility for cultural workers. In Brazil, a system of tax credits has been established which allows companies to reallocate a percentage of their income to intermediary bodies which then finance social and cultural projects—precisely one of the niches occupied by the social financing platform Benfeitoria.

## 'Pedagogical' Guidance and Workforce Education

Earlier, we noted our desire to carefully consider the antagonisms and resistances this process encounters. We must therefore call attention to a term that cropped up regularly during our interviews on both continents: 'challenge'. For instance, Christian Palouki, founder of Paydunya, explained that 'the biggest challenge' was to 'try and replicate what was already done, but also to provide education behind that'.

In fact, our studies show clearly that a significant part of the economic players' time and energy is dedicated to addressing this challenge, firstly through educational methods, and even something like agitation of those populations seen as likely to take part in crowdfunding projects. Our interviewees described the importance and frequency of workshops, online training and, above all, media presence. As the founder of Brazilian platform Catarse, Rodrigo Maia, told us: 'Public talks, presence at events: it's very good, but you have to know what you're doing.' Thameur Hemdane, co-president of the association Crowdfunding en Méditerranée, mentioned that he had taken part in various trade fairs in Africa, and explained his goal: 'We go into these spaces to preach the good news [...]. Here are the ingredients, now we'll make the recipe together.' Analogously, representatives of the ACfA claimed that, for them, it was not so much a matter of training as of educational awareness:

> This is the kind of advice I gave people in Nigeria: if you can identify people with influence who lead campaigns that touch many peoples' lives, then that's the way you can move toward a crowdfunding mentality, taking advantage of technology [...]. I don't want to wait, even though it will certainly take time, but it calls for many proactive steps.

As emphasized above, public authorities increasingly approve of this work of increasing educational awareness and agitation, even in some countries where at the moment only a minority of the population are involved in crowdfunding, and in particular the crowdfunding of cultural production. Thundafund, for example, received a two-year bursary from the South African government with the specific objective of building awareness. According to a manager of the website, the operation was beneficial insofar as 'more and more people understand the term, and each workshop received pitches from between ten and twenty people'.

On a second level, we can identify traces of more practical—more material—training activities involving different categories of players who occupy different positions in the crowdfunding production cycle. These include donors, platform managers, developers, marketers (who are more or less self-taught), and of course the multi-tasking project creators. Some of this activity may seem to go without saying, as if it constituted a normal or even 'natural' component of crowdfunding sites; but in fact it calls for an internal organization of labour that allows platforms to train their workforce. As an example, the 'project area' of Brazilian platform Benfeitoria is described as follows by its founder and manager: 'It's for project creators; *they* speak to one another and look for the best ways to direct projects, to make images, video, etc.' As illustrated in the previous chapter, in South Africa, the managers of Backabuddy, Thundafund and Citysoirée take the same approach.

Finally, there are many examples where this practical training is deployed on a more ambitious scale. These give an idea of what is strategically at stake in this 'mission', particularly in Africa. Alphabet (Google) dedicates a significant budget to regular competitions on the model of the platform Africa Connected. It aims to associate the brand and its services with the entrepreneurial projects evaluated and, in some cases, funded—with the support of international organizations like the United Nations Program for Development (UNPD) and the New Partnership for Africa's Development (NEPAD). In one such contest, the founders of the Brazilian platform Catarse received a prize from the Mountain View firm in recognition of the 'social impact' of their work (along with one million reals, according to the journalist Felipe Caruso, who has collaborated with many campaigns hosted by the platform). In the countries we studied, American ambassadors are also active in this domain. For example, they offer free or heavily discounted training to journalists and other cultural workers. Commenting on the US Embassy's use of social media, a representative of the French Embassy in Addis Ababa wrote with admiration:

> The Americans are great here. They've done some excellent work; they use Facebook all the time. Take a look, they put on courses, MOOCs, you know, open courses online, and workshops for journalists [...]. So a ballet took place and you see them talking about it. What do they do there? Workshops. Like 'Ethiopian Filmmaker'—you get training in films, in the film industry.

But it is undeniably the French ex-telecoms operator Orange that deploys the greatest effort (and the most capital) in workforce training. The following interview extract shows clearly how they put their 'pedagogy' into practice, emphasizing the supposed autonomy of the schemes financed in this way. This confirms that these strategies operate more by way of suggestion than command:

> We have a whole policy of creating incubators and accelerators […]. The two peculiarities that make them hybrid objects, to some extent, are their governance, which is a combination of public/private/civil society […]. We ask these incubators to act like startups, and to go from a pure

subsidy model to a service model in five years—that is, in the end, to construct a viable business model [...] So we've done all these experiments with Orange's money and support, but not only that, because we feel that, for the legitimacy of all of these structures, we have to open them up to others—and then that they eventually escape our control.

Similarly, in sub-Saharan Africa, Orange has invested in building and running training centres, describing them in a way that similarly foregrounds its regional legitimacy and responsibility. In the case mentioned above, in Senegal, the 'practical' pedagogy involves materially implementing the 'great discourse' of the growth of the middle-class in Africa, a mission that is clearly presented as a prerogative of this great French conglomerate (albeit not an exclusive one):

We have an educational focus: we're fairly legitimate, for example, with our coding schools, and we work with players in France [...]. Today there is a shortage of talent and skills. And our responsibility is to put in place the tools that will enable this ecosystem to be nourished. Qualified labour, the middle class, that's all of interest to us.

## Conclusion

Our research charts the emergence and extension of the use of both endogenous and exogenous social financing platforms. It illustrates the efforts made to supposedly guarantee the growth of endogenous initiatives in this domain (and beyond) when this has proved impossible through existing financial players. It also explains the proliferation of public and para-public apparatuses that offer 'flexible' guidance and support. These processes, along with 'great discourses', and a set of strategic actions, allow not only the diffusion of ideological productions (and to a certain extent their adaptation to different national contexts), but the training and organization of the various workers of the intermediation platforms.

These 'grand discourses' themselves are principally of two orders. Firstly, they promote a process of economic homogenization which depends on the emergence of what the Orange representative called the 'solvent middle class', and on its integration into an ideal globalization made possible by increased bank usage by local populations, 'good governance' and a new model of economic development in which public power takes a back seat to 'ecosystem building', within which crowdfunding must be fully integrated. The following passage gives a good summary of this discourse, all the more so if we replace the term 'firm' with 'player', so including all of the different participants mentioned above:

Firms that successfully access the monetary and non-monetary benefits of crowdfunding are found to be more competitive and more sustainable, which would be a boon for African and emerging market startup ecosystems. (InfoDev 2015: 15)

Secondly, these discourses rest upon an axiom that represents crowdfunding as an 'organic' component of a creative/digital/collaborative economy that serves the empowerment of populations 'naturally' disposed to entrepreneurship. We can see this ideology condensed in the following extract from another report on crowdfunding in Africa, which uses the term 'narrative' in a revelatory fashion:

> Crowdfunding is a major vector of African self-empowerment. Through crowdfunding, Africans have the power in their hands. The power to choose and fund social causes and economic initiatives they care about. The power to set and drive their own social and economic agenda. The power to be active and direct participants of the 'African rising' narrative. (Afrikstart 2017: 62)

These two ideological registers are obviously linked, and cannot be deployed without contradictions or without taking into account local specificities. Although a certain indifference or 'oblique attention' seems characteristic of many social actors we met during our fieldwork in sub-Saharan Africa, and who have little relation to the processes in question, a certain peculiarity of the Latin American region seems at first sight to be linked to political developments on this continent over the course of the last fifty years. Here, a version of the second discourse emerges in the form of a vision of the 'collaborative' economy as a hopeful prospect in the face of economic and political corruption—a belief in a new spirit of sharing, but one still subject to the obligation to accept 'economic realities'.

Ultimately, however, our research offered few convincing answers to the question of forms of resistance or alternatives to dominant Western logics. We met a few dissenting voices: for instance, Rodrigo Maia, cofounder of the platform Catarse, says he wants to destroy the dominant perception of how crowdfunding campaigns have to work, and to contribute to a financial transfer from the rich centres to the margins, the favelas, with the aim of 'building a more diverse country'. But this kind of discourse can also be read as ultimately opening up the platform to a more lucrative market, and remains wholly compatible with the harmonious vision of globalization advocated by the voices praising fintech.

Similarly, as in the West, we have seen micro-local projects that aim to reconnect with a more community-based spirit. Other players say they want to build bridges between so-called 'traditional' practices and tools that facilitate development. And then, among the most 'metropolitan' segments of the urban population, we can identify the expression of a desire for more authentic 'lifestyles', as illustrated by Gerhard Maree, founder of the South African platform Citysoirée, in his description of the social and cultural context in which his project first emerged:

> There was a very strong sense of a changing shift in how people wanted to consume art […] and I think we've seen that subsequently with a move

back to organic foods and, you know, supporting local economies. That people wanted to go back to the absence of corporate involvement and branded involvement. And I think that's what crowdfunding brought.

This claim associates social financing with the quest for an existence that is more ethical. But we might also ask how far this desire to short-circuit the omnipresent industrialization and commodification is, in fact, 'recuperated' by crowdfunding and its standardized processes of economic value extraction. For, as the interviewee admits: 'because of our obstinacy in remaining independent and not associating ourselves with sponsors, we haven't really made any money out of these concerts.' Tired of such paltry revenues, Gerhard Maree eventually adapted his business model, integrating the fundraising tool into a more general strategy of data collection and trading, and organization of labour—a strategy characteristic of digital intermediation platforms, as we have seen in previous chapters.

Finally we should consider a remark by Ken Aicha Sy, founder of the collective Wakh'Art de Dakar. We asked him whether the Western model of crowdfunding platforms was applicable to Africa:

> I don't think so. If it was, companies would have set up here long ago. Google is in Senegal, YouTube is in Senegal, so why not?—but I think they don't really know the market. They don't understand how the young people live, how they talk, and the same is true in Benin, Ivory Coast [...]. Even with Orange it's like that: they prefer to finance a concert by [Belgian pop musician] Stromae for €70,000 rather than three concerts a year for 10,000 CFA francs, even though that would be more popular. But Orange is a monster, and there's competition between its different departments; there's no global vision.

These comments remind us quite clearly of the limits of strategies which can indeed boast significant material power, but whose ideological effectivity remains limited due to cultural specificities—even though this phenomenon doesn't seem as yet to contribute to the emergence of clearly alternative models to Western norms.

## Notes

[1] InfoDev is describes as a 'World Bank Group program to promote entrepreneurship and innovation' http://www.infodev.org/about Accessed 5 April 2019.

[2] West African Economic and Monetary Union.

[3] Central Bank of West African States.

# References


Afrikstart. 2017. Crowdfunding in Africa: Fundraising goes Digital in Africa: The emergence of Africa-Based Crowdfunding Platforms, <http://afrikstart.com/report/wp-content/uploads/2016/09/Afrikstart-Crowdfunding-In-Africa-Report.pdf> [accessed 27 February 2019].

Bergeron, Henri, Patrick Castel and Etienne Nouguez. 2013. Éléments pour une sociologie de l'entrepreneur-frontière, *Revue française de sociologie*, 54(2), 263–302.

Comaroff, Jean, and John L. Comaroff. 2012. Theory from the South: Or, how Euro-America is evolving toward Africa, *Anthropological Forum*, 22(2), 113–131.

De Beukelaer, Christiaan. 2015. *Developing Cultural Industries: Learning from the Palimpsest of Practice*. European Cultural Foundation.

Fonds d'investissement multilatéral. 2016. *Economía colaborativa en América Latina*. Madrid: IE Business School.

Fonrouge, Cécile. 2016. Crowdfunding et diasporas: le crowdfunding vient-il bousculer les acteurs du financement diasporique?, *Actes du 13ème congrès international francophone en entrepreneuriat et PME*, <https://halshs.archives-ouvertes.fr/halshs-01392879/document> [accessed 27 February 2019].

infoDev/World Bank Group. 2015. *Crowdfunding in East Africa: Lessons from East African Start-ups*.

Jouan, Marine. 2017. *La Construction sociale du marché du crowdfunding en France* (doctoral dissertation) Telecom ParisTech.

Lapavitsas, Costas. 2009. Financialisation Embroils Developing Countries, *Papeles de Europa*, 19, 108–139.

Lobato, Ramon. 2010. Creative Industries and Informal Economies: Lessons from Nollywood, *International Journal of Cultural Studies*, 13(4), 337-354.

Nixon, Brice. 2014. Toward a Political Economy of 'Audience Labour' in the Digital Era, *Triple C*, 12(2), 713–734.

Scholz, Trebor. 2017. *Uberworked and Underpaid: How Workers are Disrupting the Digital Economy*. New York: John Wiley and Sons.

# CHAPTER 6

# General Conclusion

## Vincent Rouzé

Crowdfunding platforms are not just 'trendy' phenomena. They are symptomatic of broader ideological forms inherent to technological innovation, economic change and the emerging 'new capitalism'. As we've made clear in our second chapter, the logics of crowdfunding find their origins in a more distant and plural past, which to some extent serves to legitimize the presence and activities of contemporary platforms. The digital 'renewal' of these practices integrates somewhat diverse ideological values and conceptions. For instance, these play upon the 'gift-counter-gift' logic in order to ensure new forms of financialization of both contents and lived experiences. These same logics of  outsourcing and transfer toward citizen/consumers operate indirectly in the case of crowdsourcing and far more directly with its financial variation, crowdfunding. However, citizen and consumer participation is far from homogeneous and in this respect derides the very notion of a 'crowd', given the unequal usages among social classes in the countries where these platforms currently operate.

Our third chapter shows that, despite effectively giving visibility and economic valorisation to cultural projects that were formerly left in the shadows, these platforms must also be questioned in regard to the true alternative potential they offer. Having become new intermediaries in the cultural and creative industries, they seek to integrate and create 'ecosystems' using the might of their political, economical and technical apparatuses, which contribute to a

**How to cite this book chapter:**
Rouzé, V. 2019. General Conclusion. In: Rouzé, V. (ed.) *Cultural Crowdfunding: Platform Capitalism, Labour and Globalization.* Pp. 99–105. London: University of Westminster Press. DOI: https://doi.org/10.16997/book38.f. License: CC-BY-NC-ND 4.0

normalization of practices. Far from being the very alternatives that dominant discourses suggest, they effectively preempt concepts stemming from alternative theory and practice without engaging with its finalities. Thus, they become mere relays of broader mainstream communication and marketing logics (content individualization, self-branding, B2B and B2C match-making, personal data-mining, etc.). Beyond their apparent heterogeneity, these platforms now clearly tend toward normalization, both in terms of the rationalization of business models and externally, with regard to forms of editing, skills and actions required from project carriers and funders, as well as in terms of visibility of selected projects.

As chapter 4 shows, these platforms are reinforcing new modes of production, and indeed contributing to the tendency toward outsourced labour, in some cases 'free' labour, under the guise of both increased participation and what has been coined 'gamification'. This leads to polymorphous forms of entrepreneurship, within the organisation of platforms themselves, but also among project carriers, who have an obligation to not only seek funding but activate networks, educate and communicate in order to generate confidence and participation.

The final chapter allows us to reflect on these questions from a broader perspective. Does the development of such platforms, and the uptake of their usage, in the so-called 'Global South', correspond to (or link up with) new opportunities of emancipatory politics, diverging with the homogenizing effects of Western 'free-market' economics and forms of 'globalization' suggested by Appadurai (2001)? The results of our fieldwork in both Sub-Saharan Africa and Latin America provide some significant answers to this key question. They offer various complex examples of both compliance and resistance toward international trends, but highlight the constraints of a broadly neocolonial context within which cultural, social and economical players continue to fight out struggles which are often far removed from the simple issue of cultural crowdfunding.


## In the Service of Cultural Democratization?

These forms of cultural financing, which aim to develop individual 'creativity', also attract public and para-public institutions, which may use private platforms or develop their own. Participatory funding makes it possible to 'place cultural activity clearly at the heart of city life, as a major element in innovation, economic dynamism, attractiveness, social cohesion, and influence' (Ministère de la Culture et de la Communication 2015: 3). Ultimately, viewed this way, crowdfunding is 'without doubt a strong vector of cultural democratization and a means of reappropriating public action' (Fohr 2016: 23). If we follow this logic, will we soon see similar apparatuses emerge which allow the inhabitants of an area to directly fund a new doctor's surgery, or a new hospital? Or to finance public transport, if they live in an area abandoned by the authorities as too unprofitable? Looking past the claims of politicians and administrators who see crowdfunding as a complementary tool, rather than an exclusive one, we believe these platforms are the forerunners of logics aiming at generalized outsourcing, with activities, teams and communal and 'public' organizations funded solely by those citizens who consume them—all in the name of 'participative democracy' and a 'collaborative' economy. We should add that, while the use of crowdfunding is primarily a communication activity, it is also a way of overcoming the state's own failures using private economic logics.

## Criticism of these Innovations

Most of those who have such experiences respond with enthusiasm in the initial phases, and remain positive about them, because they met expectations which were fixed in time. But forms of discontent also become visible.

Firstly, constant involvement in the valorization process requires skills far removed from those required to launch the project. This demands time, energy and above all the possession or construction of a 'community' to support the project. Our research shows that, while people are initially very willing to use these platforms to fund their projects, those who have done so once are often hesitant to renew their project. While 83% of project creators state that they would like to use these platforms for funding, only 33% would do so for a second time.

The second concern involves the way the platforms work. MyMajorCompany and Indiegogo, for instance, have been attacked both by project creators and funders, who complain that their financial management and editorial decisions were opaque. Given the business models used, it may be that the argument that such platforms provide an alternative to the cultural industries is invalid. More recently, Patreon received heavy criticism for abruptly revising its methods for charging fees and transferring money. This is the same sort of asymmetric relationship imposed by the Big Five. It is a class relationship which favours the owners of the means of communication: the terms of service can be modified without consultation overnight.

There is also criticism of the platforms' lack of interest in providing assistance, or in offering help when litigation arises. The terms of service state clearly that these platforms are not liable in such disputes. Project creators alone are responsible. These disputes are much more frequent for technology projects. Unlike cultural projects, which are often funded by family members, technology projects attract a wider audience, without offering any guarantee of success. If a project is funded but is not completed then, regardless of the misfortunes encountered during production, the project creator will have to deal with a complaint—and do so without any hope of support from the platform.

Participation in the digital era is described as opening up a wider field of possibilities. But the tensions and contradictions noted so far raise questions about the weaknesses of such evangelism. The first of these questions is about actual citizen participation, which is often more fantasy than reality. Such participation is far from homogeneous. As with Wikipedia (Levrel 2006) or information production (Rebillard 2007), online participation is very uneven, and often follows the 1–10–100 rule: for each person active full-time, ten work only sporadically, and a further hundred merely consult what has been done by those eleven. Referring to this rule, Dominique Cardon (2010) argues that participation establishes a hierarchy between those who are very active, those who are occasionally active, and the vast majority who consult the services or content produced. Financial participation through crowdfunding follows a similar logic. Beyond a few very active funders, who the platforms emphasize and who are even recognized by the ministry of culture as 'cultural donors', financial involvement varies greatly, and is not related solely to projects.

The support which these apparatuses provide no doubt serves as a political and communicative argument for the importance ascribed to digital technologies and citizen participation. Politically, many cities (including Paris and Grenoble) have launched initiatives with participatory budgets, allowing citizens to finance selected projects. But most of these initiatives are highly fragmented and maintain the established decision-making hierarchies, creating the suspicion that participation is just a way of giving a misleading new shine to existing structures while impacting them very little, if at all. Furthermore, under the guise of emancipation and freedom, 'participatory' digital platforms act as tools of systematic control—for instance, through geolocation, the requirement to use online services, and nudging. It is no small matter that most platforms use proprietary code, far from the values of free and open source software (Smyrnaios 2018).

This leads us back to the requirement/suggestion to participate, and the need to develop effective forms of communication—for instance, educational workshops which invite as many people as possible to participate. While we are not critical of this approach in itself, we are more cautious when this participation involves the outsourcing of tasks and the shifting of financial risk onto the citizen/user/consumer alone. This marks a possible disengagement on the part of institutions and new forms of digital labour which are often 'free', breaking with hard-won legislation and social advances over the course of previous centuries. They are accompanied by educational logics which blur the lines between work and leisure, part of a process of 'gamifying society'.

Finally, there is the question of cultural diversity. The 'community' gives participation its strength, but it also marks its limit. The editorial logics which the platforms establish and community members 'put into practice' do not necessarily lead to openness and cultural diversity. Following other researchers, we have shown that the motivation for participation is based on affective proximity to the project and, often, to the person or people in charge. In such conditions, it is difficult to promote projects with aesthetic or original themes which lie on the fringes of traditional or 'mainstream' logics. Under the guise of 'participation' and freedom, the platforms valorize these disinterested, out-sourced production methods using classic capitalistic logics: data banks, big data, outsourcing tasks, and reducing investment risks. Most of them serve as new intermediaries in cultural and media strategies which have been known for decades.

Participation is therefore paradoxical: the majority of political, economic, cultural and social actors invite us to join in, but they take no responsibility for its ultimate end. In contrast to the emancipatory principles which are claimed, the participatory register is too often based on a sort of instrumentalization—one which involves nothing less than the shaping of socio-economic power relations, to the detriment of citizens and workers both nationally and internationally.

## Living in Project Mode

More generally, these platforms raise questions about the displacement of social structures in which the project becomes central. Every moment of life is governed by a project. From an early age, one has to build a life project. Students, the unemployed, academics, retirees, politicians—all must base their lives and work around the constant renewal of projects. Managers define several different project models: project companies, project portfolios, project teams, and so on (Asquin et al. 2005). Mainstream media is full of articles encouraging us to develop our economic life, our entrepreneurial life, and our personal life in 'project mode'. There are a vast number of books like Charles Smith's (2017), full of tips for succeeding in these new approaches. The challenge is to overcome all possible barriers to achieving one's goal, facing down constant challenges. 'Project planning' is defined by its unique, non-renewable nature. It involves the experiential dimension discussed above. Success depends on one's ability to master these unforeseeable events and to monitor a range of environmental constraints, all in a determined, 'irreversible' period of time. Moreover, this conception of life in project mode correlates to a dynamic aim of progress and increased action on the part of citizens.

Paradoxically, the individualization which 'project' mode brings with it is necessarily accompanied by forms of collaboration and sharing. Crowdfunding platforms valorize this project mode, and are saturated with this ideology—a genuine instance of social engineering, based on the short term, the permanent fragmentation of individual social spaces, the multiplication and diversification of skills, and permanent competition. In their own way, they track broader transformations in social structure. For this reason, as the proponents of the most retrograde social reforms claim, 'pedagogy' is necessary. Any contradiction can supposedly be dissolved with some 'educational' effort. As we have seen throughout this book, we are far from Foucault's disciplinary society: these platforms illustrate and contribute to the development of suggestions whose nature is, in reality, that of a command. These platforms seem to reject any obligation, and deploy discursive strategies where we can observe a shift towards forms of suggestion which should be followed—but without guaranteeing success for any users who comply. They participate in processes of normalization which, once accepted and naturalized, are no longer questioned. Criticising them becomes all the more complex as there is no longer any obligation—an argument used systematically by the platforms whenever criticism is raised. Lastly, crowdfunding's use of brief, short-term modalities of action denies any form of long-term commitment.

Other forms of participation and collaboration exist, some financial and others not, and these deserve more attention. They are part of the logic of the commons, of a 'commonwealth' (Hardt and Negri 2009), and serve the collective on the basis of exchanging individual resources. The relationship between proposals and participative funding would no longer be exclusively monetary, taking in broader forms of exchanging and bartering skills, places, tools, and so on. Like some forms of crowdsourcing and some 'alternative' platforms, this approach is based on pooling services which can be traded in space and time—a collective commitment where each person contributes what they want (i.e. money, skills, or time), enabling the means of production to be reappropriated (Scholz, 2016). These forms of participation invite us to overcome the difficulties and contradictions of independent initiatives—for instance, independent media initiatives (Fuchs 2014)—and so revive the links between the individual and the community. They could draw inspiration from the modalities established by the open source community, for instance, or in agriculture by 'short circuits', which often aim to produce and share their goods on the fringes of capitalist economic market logic. Such forms of participation are based on solidarity and equitable economies, and demonstrate both efficiency and a willingness to consider digital tools as a means and not an end, tying them to democratic, economic and environmental goals.

We wish to end by stressing this particular point, for we must indeed question platforms and their usages with regard to the impact they have on the environment and on global warming. So often referred to in terms of creativity, innovation, democratized usage and other such 'one-click wonders', these platforms – like all ICTs – clearly no longer correspond to the angelic expectations formulated in the 1990s (reduction in ink and paper consumption and waste, limited transport-related pollution thanks to remote working, etc.), even if they have increased knowledge transfers, exchanges and thus productivity (Rodhain and Fallery 2013). Upstream however, before we even begin to discuss either the cultural merits or the ideological threats posed by these apparatuses, we must recognise that as part of the digital economy, they require the extraction of costly raw materials, the exploitation of precarious labour, 'big data' and 'cloud' storage centres which are of course far from immaterial with regard to their high energy consumption. Downstream, the functions these platforms perform and their usages also imply ever increasing consumption of energy and contribute to climate change. Without a collective awareness and appropriate decisions on the part of all players 'participating' in this inherently reckless activity, the cultural show will go on, but until when, in what conditions and with what ultimate results?

## References


Appadurai Arjun (Ed.). 2001. *Globalization.* Durham, NC: Duke University Press.

Asquin, Alain, Christophe Falcoz and Thierry Picq. 2005. *Ce que manager par projet veut dire.* Paris: Éditions d'Organisation.

Cardon, Dominique. 2010. *La Démocratie internet: promesses et limites.* Paris: Seuil.

Fohr, Robert. 2016. Le Crowdfunding, une nouvelle forme de démocratisation culturelle?, in *Le Crowdfunding culturel,* ed. by Anaïs Del Bono and Guillaume Maréchal. Paris: Librinova.

Fuchs, Christian. 2014. Social Media and the Public Sphere, *tripleC* 12(1): 57–101.

Hardt, Michael, and Antonio Negri. 2009. *Commonwealth.* Cambridge, MA: Harvard University Press.

Levrel, Julien. 2006. Wikipedia, un dispositif médiatique de publics participants, *Réseaux,* 138.4, 185–218, http://www.cairn.info/revue-reseaux1-2006-4-page-185.html [last accessed 5 March 2019].

Ministère de la Culture et de la Communication. 2015. *Signature de protocoles pour le développement du mécénat culturel.* Available at: http://www.culture.gouv.fr/content/download/128681/1405955/version/1/file> [ last accessed 5 April 2019].

Rebillard, Franck. 2007. *Le web 2.0 en perspective: une analyse socio-économique de l'internet.* Paris: L'Harmattan.

Rodhain Florence and Bernard Fallery. 2013. ICT and Ecology: In Favour of Research Based on the Responsibility Principle. Mediterranean Conference of Information Systems, Athens, Greece. 173–186.

Scholz, Trebor. 2016. *Platform Cooperativism. Challenging the Corporate Sharing Economy.* New York: Rosa Luxemburg Foundation.

Smith, Charles. 2017. *Making Sense of Project Realities: Theory, Practice and the Pursuit of Performance.* Abingdon: Routledge.

Smyrnaios, Nikos. 2018. *Internet Oligopoly: The Corporate Takeover of Our Digital World.* Bingley: Emerald.

# The Editor and Contributors

## Competing Interests

All the chapters in this book are the result of research carried out within the framework of the Collab research project, financed by the French National Research Agency (ANR) and directed by Vincent Rouzé (2015–18). This publication was made possible thanks to the support of the ANR, University Paris 8, CEMTI and the University of Westminster Press.

## The Editor and Contributors

**Vincent Rouzé** is Associate Professor of Information and Communication Sciences at the University of Paris 8 and a member of the Centre for Media, Technology and Internationalization Studies (Cemti). Author of numerous articles, his work deals with musical and artistic practices with regard to digital technologies and the evolution of their methods of valorization and circulation. He has participated in and directed research programmes related to those matters and was the leader of the 'Collab' research programme (2015–18) funded by the French National Research Agency. He is the author of *Mythologie de l'iPod* (2010), co-author of *La Culture par les Foules* (2014) and coedited the volume *Financement Participatif: les Nouveaux Territoires du Capitalisme* (2019). Email: vincent.rouze@univ-paris8.fr

**Jacob Matthews** is Professor of Information and Communication Sciences at the University of Paris 8, France. He is the author of *Communication d'une Star, Jim Morrison* (2003), co-author of *Le Web Collaboratif* (2010), *La Culture par les Foules* (2014) and *Platform Economics* (2018). He has directed several research programmes looking into evolutions in the culture industries and the development of the collaborative web and was head of the Centre for Media, Technology and Internationalization Studies (Cemti) in 2017–18. He is currently an associate member of the Laboratory of Applied Research in Social Sciences (Lerass, University of Toulouse 3) and the Inter-university Research Centre on Communication, Information and Society (Cricis, University of Quebec in

Montreal). His research now primarily focuses on the political economy of the Internet and digital intermediation platforms.
Email: jacob.matthews@univ-paris8.fr

**Stéphane Costantini** holds a PhD in Information and Communication Sciences and is an associate researcher at the University of Paris 13. He was a research engineer within the 'Collab' research programme (2015–18). His work in the area of socioeconomy of cultural and communication industries, focuses on the strategies of industrial players and user practices in the field of digital and collaborative web, as well as the uses of amateurs and professionals in the music world. A decade of professional experience in the field of cultural communication (music, audiovisual, theatre, copyright) has enabled him to cross-reference the views of cultural and digital professionals with academic research.
Email: steph.costantini@gmail.com

**Alix Bénistant** holds a PhD in Information and Communication Sciences, and is an associate researcher at the Centre for Media, Technology and Internationalization Studies (Cemti, University of Paris 8) and at the Research Centre on Mediations (Crem, University of Lorraine), where he was a research fellow in the 'Collab' research programme. His current research concerns the production and circulation of cultural products on a transnational scale, and the role played by large metropolitan areas in the context of globalization. His field of analysis focuses more specifically on the music industry that has settled in the city of Miami.
E-mail: alix.benistant@gmail.com

Printed and bound by CPI Group (UK) Ltd, Croydon, CR0 4YY

07/07/2026

14916228-0003